Fix It!® Grammar

Mowgli and Shere Khan

STUDENT BOOK
LEVEL 4

Pamela White

Fourth Edition, January 2022
Institute for Excellence in Writing, L.L.C.

Contributors
Sabrina Cardinale
Heidi Thomas
Denise Kelley

Designer
Melanie Anderson

Instructions

The list below shows the components to each *Fix It! Grammar* weekly exercise.

Although **Mark It** is listed before **Fix It**, the student may choose to **Fix It** first and then **Mark It**. This is acceptable because the *Fix It! Grammar* exercises are like a word puzzle. The goal is to complete the lists at the top of the student page for each passage.

Students should discuss their work with the teacher after working through each daily passage. However, older students may work with their teacher on a weekly basis. Students should actively be involved in comparing their work with the Teacher's Manual. The repetition of finding and fixing their own mistakes allows them to recognize and avoid those mistakes in the future.

Fix It! Grammar should be treated as a game. Keep it fun!

Editing Marks

¶   indent

∧   insert

⌐   delete

⟝   capitalize

✗   lowercase

⌣   reverse order

add a space

⌒   close the space

Learn It!	On the first day of the new Week, read through the Learn It section. Each Learn It covers a concept that the student will practice in future passages. Instructions for marking and fixing passages are included in each Learn It.
Read It!	Read the day's passage.
	Look up the bolded vocabulary word in a dictionary and pick the definition that fits the context of the story. Maintain a list of vocabulary words and their definitions.
	The vocabulary definitions are printed in the Teacher's Manual.
Mark It!	Mark the passage using the guide at the top of the daily practice page.
Fix It!	Correct the passage using the guide at the top of the daily practice page.
	The Teacher's Manual includes detailed explanations for grammar concepts and punctuation in each daily passage.
Rewrite It!	After marking, correcting, and discussing the passage with the teacher, copy the corrected passage on the lines provided or into a separate notebook.

Helpful Hints

Use different colors for **Mark It** and **Fix It**.

- Copy the corrected story, not the editing marks.
- Indent and use capital letters properly.
- Copy the corrected punctuation.

Appendix I Complete Story Familiarize yourself with the story that you will be editing by reading the complete story found in Appendix I.

Appendix II Collection Pages Look for strong verbs, quality adjectives, and -ly adverbs in this book and write them on the collection pages in Appendix II.

Appendix III Lists Refer to the lists found in Appendix III to quickly identify pronouns, prepositions, verbs, and conjunctions.

Appendix IV Grammar Glossary Reference the Grammar Glossary found in Appendix IV of the Teacher's Manual for more information about the concepts taught in the *Fix It! Grammar* series.

Fix It! Grammar Cards are an optional product that will enhance the *Fix It! Grammar* learning experience.

Fix It! Grammar Cards

Thirty full color grammar cards highlight key *Fix It! Grammar* concepts for quick and easy reference.

For a more relaxed and entertaining way to drill and review grammar concepts learned, instructions for a download of multiple game ideas are included in the card pack.

Fix It! Grammar Cards are beautifully designed and come in a sturdy card box for easy storage.

IEW.com/FIX-GC

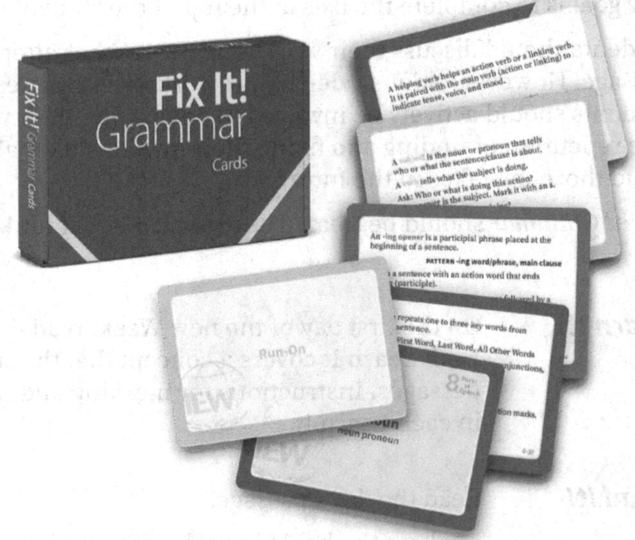

On the chart below *Fix It! Grammar Cards* are listed in the order that the information is taught in this book. Some cards are not introduced until future books.

WEEK	Fix It! Grammar Cards for *Mowgli and Shere Khan* Level 4
1	Editing Marks, Indentation, Capitalization, Title, Noun, Pronoun, Preposition, Number Words and Numerals
2	Subject-Verb Pair, Clause, Verb, Linking Verb, Helping Verb, Sentence Openers
3	Conjunction, Coordinating Conjunction, Prepositional Phrase
4	Adjective, Dependent Clause, Quotation
5	Adverb, #3 -ly Adverb Opener, www Word
6	Apostrophes, Indefinite Pronoun
8	Run-On
9	Interjection
13	#4 -ing Opener
17	Commas with Adjectives before a Noun
Not Used	Comparative and Superlative Adjectives and Adverbs

Scope and Sequence

Week numbers indicate when a concept is introduced or specifically reinforced in a lesson. Once introduced the concept is practiced throughout the book.

Parts of Speech

Week	1	2	3	4	5	6	7	8	9	10	11	12	13	14	15	16	17	18	19	20	21	22	23	24	25	26	27	28	29	30
Noun	1																													
subject noun		2																												
noun of direct address										10																				
plural noun						6																								
Pronoun	1	2																												
personal pronoun	1																													
subject pronoun		2			5				9																					
indefinite pronoun						6	7																							
possessive pronoun				4			7																							
demonstrative pronoun							7																							
reflexive pronoun	1							8																						
interrogative pronoun					5							12																		
unclear pronoun																												28		
Preposition	1												13	14																
Verb																														
action verb		2																												
linking verb		2																												
helping verb		2																												
phrasal verb			3																											
subject/verb agreement						6			9																					
verb tense							7				11																			
verb phrase											11					16														
Conjunction			3																	20										
coordinating			3							10										20										
subordinating											11									20										
Adjective				4																										
article adjective	1																													
possessive adjective				4		6		8																						
coordinate adjectives																		18							25					
cumulative adjectives																	17								25					
compound adjective																										26				
Adverb					5																									
interrogative adverb									9																					
Interjection									9																					

	Week	1	2	3	4	5	6	7	8	9	10	11	12	13	14	15	16	17	18	19	20	21	22	23	24	25	26	27	28	29	30

Capitalization

	1	2	3	4	5	6	7	8	9	10	11	12	13	14	15	16	17	18	19	20	21	22	23	24	25	26	27	28	29	30
First Word of Sentence	1																													
Proper Noun	1																													
Proper Adjective	1																													
Personal Pronoun I	1																													
Interjection									9																					
Quotation Marks				4		6																								

Punctuation

End Marks

	1	2	3	4	5	6	7	8	9	10	11	12	13	14	15	16	17	18	19	20	21	22	23	24	25	26	27	28	29	30
period	1																													
question mark	1																													
exclamation mark	1				5				9																					
quotation marks				4	5																									

Commas

	1	2	3	4	5	6	7	8	9	10	11	12	13	14	15	16	17	18	19	20	21	22	23	24	25	26	27	28	29	30
a and b			3							10																				
a, b, and c			3							10																				
MC, cc MC									9	10																				
prepositional phrase			3											14		16														
who/which clause				4															19											
quotations				4																										
that clause							7																23							
interjection									9															24						
noun of direct address										10																				
#2 prepositional opener			3											14	15	16														
#3 -ly adverb opener					5										15															
adverb clause											11																			
#5 clausal opener					5						11				15															
comma splice								8	9																					
cumulative adjectives																	17								25					
coordinate adjectives																		18							25					
#4 -ing opener													13		15	16					21									
unnecessary commas																								24					29	

Quotation Marks

	1	2	3	4	5	6	7	8	9	10	11	12	13	14	15	16	17	18	19	20	21	22	23	24	25	26	27	28	29	30
Quotation Marks				4		6																								

Apostrophes

	1	2	3	4	5	6	7	8	9	10	11	12	13	14	15	16	17	18	19	20	21	22	23	24	25	26	27	28	29	30
contraction						6																								
possessive adjective						6		8																						

Hyphens

	1	2	3	4	5	6	7	8	9	10	11	12	13	14	15	16	17	18	19	20	21	22	23	24	25	26	27	28	29	30
compound adjective																										26				

	Week	1	2	3	4	5	6	7	8	9	10	11	12	13	14	15	16	17	18	19	20	21	22	23	24	25	26	27	28	29	30

Clauses

	1	2	3	4	5	6	7	8	9	10	11	12	13	14	15	16	17	18	19	20	21	22	23	24	25	26	27	28	29	30
Who/Which Clause				4								12							19		21	22								
That Clause							7					12											23							
Adverb Clause					5						11	12		14																
Dependent Clause				4			7				11	12											23							
Main Clause		2										12															27			

Phrases

	1	2	3	4	5	6	7	8	9	10	11	12	13	14	15	16	17	18	19	20	21	22	23	24	25	26	27	28	29	30
prepositional phrase	1		3										13	14		16														
verb phrase											11					16														
participial (-ing) phrase													13			16					21						27			

Homophones

	1	2	3	4	5	6	7	8	9	10	11	12	13	14	15	16	17	18	19	20	21	22	23	24	25	26	27	28	29	30
Whose/Who's																						22								

Other Concepts

	1	2	3	4	5	6	7	8	9	10	11	12	13	14	15	16	17	18	19	20	21	22	23	24	25	26	27	28	29	30
Indentation	1																													
Numbers	1																													
Subject-Verb Pairs		2																						24						
Fused Sentence								8	9																					
Comma Splice								8	9																					
Imperative Sentence					5																									
Usage																														
pronoun agreement		2	3	4																		22								
adverb/adjective					5																									
subject/verb agreement						6			9																					
verb tense							7				11																			
reflexive pronoun								8																						
who/whom/whose																					21	22								

Stylistic Techniques

	1	2	3	4	5	6	7	8	9	10	11	12	13	14	15	16	17	18	19	20	21	22	23	24	25	26	27	28	29	30
Strong Verb		2																												
Quality Adjective				4																										
Who/Which Clause				4								12							19		21	22								
-ly Adverb					5																									
Adverb Clause					5						11	12		14																
#1 Subject Opener		2													15															
#2 Prepositional Opener			3											14	15															
#3 -ly Adverb Opener					5										15															
#4 -ing Opener													13		15	16					21									
#5 Clausal Opener											11				15															
#6 Vss Opener										10					15															

Vocabulary

1 vast lame limit endanger	**2** desperate strayed alerted retaliate	**3** apprehension puny entrance glared	**4** pack frustration boldness practical	**5** annual squatting threatened considerably	**6** addressed claim purchase preserve
7 eagerly thickly detect leisure	**8** awkwardly carefree gaze occasions	**9** mistrusted craftily content embarrassed	**10** urgently shrugged concerned manipulates	**11** aggressive hesitated reasoned oblivious	**12** jagged bore captivity miserably
13 blow cautiously distress steadily	**14** intensely accomplish responded recognize	**15** potential dread anxiously taunted	**16** kill descending crouched unfamiliar	**17** mist concluded astounded constantly	**18** hailed senseless inevitably blossomed
19 capable ascended clutched challenging	**20** clumsy tension wearily approach	**21** solitary succulent recently menacingly	**22** decade vows protested maintained	**23** influenced restored consider furiously	**24** murmuring inwardly cease comprehend
25 igniting cowering consistently quivered	**26** pledged betray debt frantically	**27** confidently tolerate commanded respected	**28** peering struck dusk blurted	**29** confused confirm determined sorrow	**30** pleading generosity kin varied

Contents

Appendices

Learn It!

Every word belongs to a word group—a part of speech. There are eight parts of speech: noun, pronoun, verb, preposition, conjunction, adjective, adverb, interjection.

8 Parts of Speech

Noun

A **noun** names a person, place, thing, or idea.

A **compound noun** is two or more words combined to form a single noun. This includes proper nouns with two or more words, such as *Shere Khan*.

Noun

Definition:
A noun names a person, place, thing, or idea.

Tests:

the   _________

two   _________

Article Adjective

The **article adjectives** are *a, an, the.* A noun follows an article adjective.

Pronoun

A **pronoun** replaces a noun in order to avoid repetition. It refers back to some person or thing recently mentioned known as the antecedent. Review the types of pronouns in Appendix III.

A **personal pronoun** takes the place of common and proper nouns.

A **reflexive pronoun** ends in -self (singular) or -selves (plural) and refers to the subject of the same sentence.

Pronoun

Definition:
A pronoun replaces a noun in order to avoid repetition.

List: Appendix III

Preposition

A **preposition** starts a phrase that shows the relationship between a noun or pronoun and another word in the sentence. A prepositional phrase *always* begins with a preposition and ends with a noun or pronoun (called the object of the preposition). Review the prepositions in Appendix III.

Preposition

Definition:
A preposition starts a phrase that shows the relationship between a noun or pronoun and another word in the sentence.

Memorize It!   **preposition + noun (no verb)**

Mark It!   Write *n* above each noun. Use a single *n* for a compound noun.
Write *ar* above each article and *pr* above each pronoun.
Underline each prepositional phrase.

Pattern:
preposition + noun (no verb)

List: Appendix III

```
     n                        pr    ar        n      ar   n
Shere Khan considered himself the greatest beast in the jungle.
```

Numbers

Spell out numbers that can be expressed in one or two words, like *twelve* and *one hundred*.

Use a hyphen with numbers from twenty-one to ninety-nine.

Spell out ordinal numbers, like *first* and *second*.

Ordinal numbers tell the order or position in a sequence.

Fix It!   Place a line through the incorrect number and write the correct word above it.

```
                 six                                    seventh
Mother Wolf had 6 cubs. Mowgli would become her 7th.
```

Capitalization

Capitalize the first word of a sentence.

Capitalize proper nouns and proper adjectives.

Capitalize the personal pronoun *I*.

End Mark

Use a period at the end of a statement.

Use a question mark at the end of a question.

Use an exclamation mark at the end of a sentence that expresses strong emotion.

Indentation

An **indentation** is a blank space between the margin and the beginning of a line of text. It shows the start of a new paragraph.

In fiction (stories), there are four reasons to start a new paragraph.

New Speaker: Start a new paragraph when a new character speaks. Include the attribution with the quotation. Sentences before or after the quotation that point directly to the quotation can remain in the same paragraph.

New Topic: Start a new paragraph when the narrator or a character switches the topic.

New Place: Start a new paragraph when the story switches to a new location. If several switches are made in quick succession, such as a character's journey to find something, it may be less choppy to keep in one paragraph.

New Time: Start a new paragraph when the time changes.

Fix It! Place three short lines below letters that should be capitalized.
Place the correct end mark at the end of each sentence.
Add the ¶ symbol or an arrow ➔ in front of each sentence that should start a new paragraph.

¶ shere khan killed some of the villagers' cows. the villagers were enraged!

When you rewrite the passage, indent. Start the sentence on the next line and write ½ inch from the left margin.

Learn It!

Verb

A **verb** shows action, links the subject to another word, or helps another verb.

An **action verb** shows action or ownership.

A **linking verb** links the subject to a noun or adjective.

A **helping verb** helps an action verb or a linking verb. The helping verb is always followed by another verb.

Every verb has a subject. The subject and verb (s v) belong together.

Subject

A **subject** is a noun or pronoun that performs a verb action. It tells who or what the clause is about.

Clause

A **clause** is a group of related words that contains both a subject and a verb.

Main Clause

A **main clause** contains a subject and a verb and expresses a complete thought, so it can stand alone as a sentence. Every sentence must have a main clause.

Find It!   Read the sentence and look for the verb.
Ask, "Who or what ____ (verb)?"

Mark It!   Write *v* above each verb and *s* above each subject.
Place square brackets around the main clause *[MC]*.

      s   *v*

[The tiger knew the laws of the jungle].

Sentence Opener

A **sentence opener** is a descriptive word, phrase, or clause that is added to the beginning of a sentence. Using different sentence openers makes writing more interesting. After you mark a sentence, determine if the sentence begins with an opener that you know. If it does, mark it. Do not mark questions or quoted sentences.

#1 Subject Opener

A **#1 subject opener** is a sentence that begins with the subject of the sentence. Sometimes, an article or adjective will come before the subject, but the sentence is still a #1 subject opener.

Mark It!   Write ①above the first word of a sentence that starts with a subject opener.

①   *s*   *v*

A young boy wandered from his village.

---

8 Parts of Speech

Verb

Definition:
A verb shows action, links the subject to another word, or helps another verb.

Verb Test:

I _____ .

It _____ .

Linking Verbs

am, is, are, was, were, be, being, been, seem, become, appear, grow, remain, taste, sound, smell, feel, look

Helping Verbs

am, is, are, was, were, be, being, been, have, has, had, do, does, did, may, might, must, can, will, shall, could, would, should

Verb Lists:
Appendix III

Strong Verb

A **strong verb** dresses up writing because it creates a strong image or feeling. A strong verb is an action verb, never a linking or helping verb. Look for strong verbs in this book and write them on the Strong Verb collection page, Appendix II.

Usage with Pronoun Agreement

A **pronoun** replaces a noun in order to avoid repetition. An **antecedent** is the word the pronoun refers to.

The boy wandered. He did not hear his mother call him.

The personal pronouns *he, his,* and *him* refer to the noun *boy.* The noun *boy* is the antecedent of the pronouns *he, his,* and *him.*

A personal pronoun should agree with its antecedent in number.

Number means one (singular) or more than one (plural).

		Subjective	Objective	Possessive	
2 numbers					
singular	*1st*	I	me	my	mine
	2nd	you	you	your	yours
	3rd	he, she, it	him, her, it	his, her, its	his, hers, its
plural	*1st*	we	us	our	ours
	2nd	you	you	your	yours
	3rd	they	them	their	theirs

The boy wandered. He did not hear his mother call him.

Boy refers to one boy. Therefore, only the pronouns in the singular row can replace the word *boy.*

The boys wandered. They did not hear their mother call them.

Boys refers to more than one boy. Therefore, only the pronouns in the plural row can replace the word *boys.*

Throughout this book you will see usage errors.

Fix It!   Place a line through the incorrect pronoun and write the correct pronoun above it.

They

The wolves obeyed the law. ~~He~~ could endanger others if

they   *He*

~~she~~ did not. A wolf learned the law as a cub. ~~They~~ obeyed

it always.

Learn It!

Conjunction

A **conjunction** connects words, phrases, or clauses. A **coordinating conjunction** connects the same type of words, phrases, or clauses. The items must be grammatically the same: two or more adjectives, two or more prepositional phrases, and so forth.

Comma

Do not use a comma before a coordinating conjunction when it connects two items in a series unless they are main clauses. **PATTERN a and b**

Use commas to separate three or more items in a series. **PATTERN a, b, and c**

Mark It!   Write **cc** above each coordinating conjunction.

Fix It!   Insert or remove commas. Follow the comma rules.

The toddler was lively, but defenseless.

He climbed a hill, peeked inside the cave, and wandered in.

#2 Prepositional Opener

A **#2 prepositional opener** is a sentence that begins with a prepositional phrase. The first word in the sentence must be a preposition.

Comma

If a prepositional opener has five words or more, follow it with a comma.

If two or more prepositional phrases open a sentence, follow the last phrase with a comma.

Do not put a comma in front of a prepositional phrase.

Mark It!   Write ② above the first word of a sentence that starts with a prepositional phrase.

Fix It!   Insert or remove commas. Follow the comma rules.

② Inside the cave, the wolf cubs wrestled, with their mother.

② Inside the dark and dank cave, the wolf cubs wrestled.

Do not include the opener in the main clause square brackets.

② From the entrance of the cave, [Father Wolf watched].

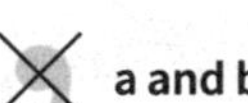

Coordinating Conjunction

Definition: A coordinating conjunction connects the same type of words, phrases, or clauses.

FANBOYS

for, and, nor, but, or, yet, so

a and b

a, b, and c

Pattern:

preposition + noun (no verb)

Phrasal Verbs

A **phrasal verb** functions as a single verb but has another word with the verb. The combined words form an idea that is different from the two individual words.

> To *cry* means to shed tears; *out* means away from. To *cry out* does not mean to weep away from but to shout something. *Cry out* is a phrasal verb.

Mark It!   Write a single *v* above a phrasal verb.

The boy could not catch up with the wolves.

Usage with Pronoun Agreement

A **pronoun** replaces a noun.

An **antecedent** is the word the pronoun refers to.

Week 2 you learned that a pronoun should agree with its antecedent in number (singular and plural). It should also agree with its antecedent in person.

Person means who is speaking (1st), spoken to (2nd), or spoken about (3rd).

2 numbers	3 persons	Subjective	Objective	Possessive	
singular	1st	I	me	my	mine
singular	2nd	you	you	your	yours
singular	3rd	he, she, it	him, her, it	his, her, its	his, hers, its
plural	1st	we	us	our	ours
plural	2nd	you	you	your	yours
plural	3rd	they	them	their	theirs

I did not hear my mother call me.

A character is **speaking** about himself. The speaker uses pronouns in the first-person row to speak about himself.

You did not hear your mother call you.

A character is **spoken to**. The speaker uses pronouns in the second-person row to speak to someone else.

He did not hear his mother call him.

A character is **spoken about**. The speaker uses pronouns in the third-person row to speak about another character.

Fix It!   Place a line through the incorrect pronoun and write the correct pronoun above it.

The wolf cubs ignored Shere Khan. ~~You~~ *He* could not scare ~~us~~ *them*.

Read It!	**Mark It!**	**Fix It!**
1 vocabulary	3 articles (ar)	4 capitals
	6 nouns (n)	3 commas
	1 pronoun (pr)	1 end mark
	2 coordinating conjunctions (cc)	1 number
	2 prepositional phrases	1 usage
	2 [main clauses]	
	2 subject-verb pairs (s v)	
	2 openers	

with great **apprehension**, father wolf paced.

a small hairless creature wandered into the shallow

cave, and joined the 6 cubs, and our mother

Rewrite It! ____

____

____

____

____

Read It!	**Mark It!**	**Fix It!**	Day 2
1 vocabulary	2 articles (ar)	4 capitals	
	5 nouns (n)	1 end mark	
	1 pronoun (pr)	3 commas	
	3 <u>prepositional phrases</u>	1 usage	
	2 [main clauses]		
	2 subject-verb pairs (s v)		
	2 openers		

until that day, father wolf had never seen a man's cub.

they stared, in amazement, at the **puny** child

Rewrite It! ____

____

____

____

____

| **Read It!** | **Mark It!** | **Fix It!** | |

Read It!

1 vocabulary

Mark It!

4 articles (ar)
6 nouns (n)
1 pronoun (pr)
1 coordinating conjunction (cc)
4 prepositional phrases
2 [main clauses]
2 subject-verb pairs (s v)
2 openers

Fix It!

1 indent
4 capitals
2 commas
1 end mark
1 usage

without any warning, shere khan appeared at the

entrance of the cave, but could not fit through

the opening. you wanted the man's cub to come out

Rewrite It! ____

____

____

____

____

Read It!	**Mark It!**	**Fix It!**
1 vocabulary	2 nouns (n)	1 indent
	3 pronouns (pr)	6 capitals
	1 coordinating conjunction (cc)	2 commas
	1 <u>prepositional phrase</u>	1 end mark
	3 [main clauses]	1 usage
	3 subject-verb pairs (s v)	
	3 openers	

mother wolf shook herself. she stood up snarled

and **glared** at shere khan. i was furious

Rewrite It! ____

____

____

____

____

Learn It!

Adjective

An **adjective** describes a noun or pronoun. It can come before the noun it describes (*young* boy), or it can follow a linking verb and describe the subject of the clause (boy was *young*).

Possessive Adjective

A **possessive adjective** shows ownership. It answers the question *whose*. When a noun is followed by an apostrophe + *s*, it functions as a possessive adjective. In the same way, the possessive pronouns *my, your, his, her, its, our, their* function as possessive adjectives.

Mark It!   Write *adj* above each adjective.

    adj   *adj* *adj*   *adj*

The wolf's desire to protect her young cubs was instinctive.

Quality Adjective

A **quality adjective** dresses up writing because it creates a strong image or feeling. Look for quality adjectives in this book and write them on the Quality Adjective collection page, Appendix II.

Who/Which Clause

A **who/which clause** is a dependent clause that begins with the word *who* or *which*. It is an adjective clause because it follows the noun it describes. Use the pronoun *who* when referring to people, personified animals, and pets. Use the pronoun *which* when referring to things, animals, and places.

The subject of most *who/which* clauses is *who* or *which*, but sometimes the subject is another word in the clause.

Comma

Place commas around a *who/which* clause if it is nonessential.

Do not place commas around a *who/which* clause if it is essential (changes the meaning of the sentence).

Mark It!   Place parentheses around the *who/which* clause and write *w/w* above the word *who* or *which*. Write *v* above each verb and *s* above each subject.

Fix It!   Insert commas around a nonessential *who/which* clause.

                              w/w   *s*   *v*

Mowgli had a bold spirit**,** (which the wolves admired**)**.

Weeks 4–18 contain only nonessential *who/which* clauses. They require commas. Week 19 you will learn how to determine if a clause is essential or nonessential. Week 21 you will learn when a *who/which* clause should begin with *whom* or *whose*.

---

8 Parts of Speech

Adjective

Definition:
An adjective describes a noun or pronoun.

Test:
  the ___ pen

Questions:
  which one?
  what kind?
  how many?
  whose?

Dependent **C**lause

Who/Which Clause

Contains:
subject + verb

First Word:
who or which

Commas:
unless essential

Marking:
w/w

Quotation Marks—Capitalization and End Marks

Quotation marks indicate words are spoken. The quote is the sentence in quotation marks.
The attribution is the person speaking and the speaking verb.

Comma

Attribution, "Quote."

"Quote," attribution.

"Quote," attribution,
"rest of quoted
sentence."

Attribution, "Quote?"

"Quote?" attribution.

Attribution, "Quote!"

"Quote!" attribution.

Use a comma to separate an attribution from a direct quote.

Fix It!   Place quotation marks around the words that are spoken.
Place three short lines below letters that should be capitalized.
Place the correct end mark at the end of each sentence.
Place a comma between an attribution and a quote.

mother wolf insisted, "leave this place!"

"i will get him in the end," the tiger snarled.

Usage with Pronoun Agreement

A personal pronoun should agree with its antecedent in number, person, and case.

Case refers to the way a pronoun functions in a sentence.

3 cases		*Subjective* function as	*Objective* function as	*Possessive* function as	
		subject subject complement	object of preposition direct object indirect object	adjective	pronoun
2 numbers	3 persons				
singular	1st	I	me	my	mine
	2nd	you	you	your	yours
	3rd	he, she, it	him, her, it	his, her, its	his, hers, its
plural	1st	we	us	our	ours
	2nd	you	you	your	yours
	3rd	they	them	their	theirs

If a pronoun functions as a subject, use a subjective case pronoun. If a pronoun follows
a preposition and functions as the object of the preposition, use an objective case
pronoun. If a pronoun describes a noun, use a possessive case pronoun that functions
as an adjective.

Fix It!   Place a line through the incorrect pronoun and write the correct pronoun
above it.

Mowgli enjoyed the cubs. His played with they in theirs cave.

Read It!	**Mark It!**	**Fix It!**
1 vocabulary	3 articles (ar)	4 capitals
	3 nouns (n)	5 commas
	5 pronouns (pr)	2 quotation marks
	2 coordinating conjunctions (cc)	1 end mark
	1 adjective (adj)	1 usage
	2 <u>prepositional phrases</u>	
	4 [main clauses]	
	1 *who/which* clause (w/w)	
	5 subject-verb pairs (s v)	
	1 opener	

she growled the man's cub who is now mine

lives here! him shall run, with the **pack** and hunt

with the pack. he will grow up, and hunt you

Rewrite It! ____

____

____

____

____

Read It!	**Mark It!**	**Fix It!**	
			Day 2

Read It!	**Mark It!**	**Fix It!**
1 vocabulary	1 article (ar)	1 indent
	7 nouns (n)	4 capitals
	4 adjectives (adj)	3 commas
	3 <u>prepositional phrases</u>	1 end mark
	2 [main clauses]	1 number
	1 *who/which* clause (w/w)	1 usage
	3 subject-verb pairs (s v)	
	2 openers	

shere khan who had lost the argument left, in

frustration. mother wolf planned to raise this

man's cub in addition to my 6 cubs

Rewrite It! ____

____

____

____

Read It! | **Mark It!** | **Fix It!**

1 vocabulary

6 nouns (n)
4 pronouns (pr)
1 coordinating conjunction (cc)
7 adjectives (adj)
2 <u>prepositional phrases</u>
2 [main clauses]
1 *who/which* clause (w/w)
3 subject-verb pairs (s v)
2 openers

3 capitals
4 commas
1 end mark
2 usage

because of his looks, she named him mowgli which

means frog. she loved he for his unusual **boldness**

their comical expressions and his playful spirit

Rewrite It!

Read It!	**Mark It!**	**Fix It!**	Day 4
1 vocabulary	1 article (ar)	4 capitals	
	5 nouns (n)	1 end mark	
	1 pronoun (pr)	2 commas	
	3 adjectives (adj)	1 number	
	3 prepositional phrases	1 usage	
	2 [main clauses]		
	1 *who/which* clause (w/w)		
	3 subject-verb pairs (s v)		
	2 openers		

father wolf who was more **practical** feared for

mowgli's acceptance. him would need approval

from 2 members of the pack

Rewrite It! ____

____

____

____

Learn It!

Adverb

An **adverb** modifies a verb, an adjective, or another adverb. An adverb often ends in -ly. However, many adverbs do not, including *very, together, never, soon*. The words *yes, no, not, too, even,* and *else* also function as adverbs.

Mark It!   Write *adv* above each adverb.

    adv   *adv*

Mowgli quietly played. The wolves would soon decide his fate.

-ly Adverb

An **-ly adverb** dresses up writing when it creates a strong image or feeling. Look for -ly adverbs in this book and write them on the -ly Adverb collection page, Appendix II.

Usage with Adverbs and Adjectives

Both adverbs and adjectives add detail to a sentence. Adverbs modify verbs, adjectives, and other adverbs, while adjectives describe nouns and pronouns. Use the adverb and adjective questions to determine how a word functions in a sentence.

Mark It!   Write *adv* above each adverb and *adj* above each adjective.

Fix It!   Place a line through the incorrect word and write the correct word above it.

  adj   *adv*
restless   furiously

The ~~restlessly~~ tiger switched his tail ~~furious~~.

#3 -ly Adverb Opener

A **#3 -ly adverb** opener is a sentence that begins with an -ly adverb.

Comma

, Use a comma if an -ly adverb opener modifies the sentence.

✗ Do not use a comma if an -ly adverb opener modifies the verb.

To determine if an -ly adverb modifies the sentence, test it: It was ＿＿ that ＿＿.

If this makes sense, the -ly adverb is a sentence adverb. Use a comma.

If this does not make sense, confirm that the -ly adverb modifies the verb. Do not use a comma.

Mark It!   Write ③ above the first word of a sentence that starts with an -ly adverb.

Fix It!   Insert or remove commas. Follow the comma rules.

③   -ly

Obviously, Mowgli was content.

③   -ly

Comfortably, Mowgli sat in the dirt.

Parts of Speech

Adverb

Definition:
An adverb modifies a verb, an adjective, or another adverb.

Questions:
 how?
 when?
 where?
 why?
 to what extent?

Adverb Clause

Pattern:
www word +
subject + verb

First Word:
www word

Commas:
after, not before

Marking:
AC

Attribution, "Quote?"
"Quote?" attribution.

Attribution, "Quote!"
"Quote!" attribution.

Adverb Clause

An **adverb clause** is a dependent clause that begins with a www word and contains a subject and a verb.

Memorize It!   www word + subject + verb

Use the acronym *www.asia.b* to remember the eight most common www words.

Memorize It!

w	w	w	a	s	i	a	b
when	while	where	as	since	if	although	because

Mark It!   Place parentheses around the adverb clause and write *AC* above the www word. Write *v* above each verb and *s* above each subject.

AC   s   v
(Although he was furious**)**, he could not grab Mowgli
AC   s   v
(while the wolves watched**)**.

Quotations with End Marks

Week 4 you learned that a comma separates an attribution from a quote. When a quoted sentence asks a question or expresses strong emotion, place the question or exclamation mark inside the closing quotations.

"Who is this**?"** the cubs asked. "He has no fur**!"** they yelled.

The question or exclamation mark replaces the comma. If an attribution comes after a quotation, the first word of the attribution is not capitalized.

Imperative Sentence (Implied Subject)

An **imperative sentence** gives a command or makes a request. Because commands are always directed toward someone, the subject of an imperative sentence is always *you*.

Mark It!   Write **(you)** in parentheses to show the subject of an imperative sentence. Write *v* above each verb and *s* above *you*.

s   v
(you) Play quietly.

Interrogative Pronoun

An **interrogative pronoun** is used to ask a question. The most common interrogative pronouns are *what, whatever, which, whichever, who, whoever, whom, whose.*

Mark It!   Write *pr* above each pronoun.

pr   pr
What will the pack decide? Who will speak for Mowgli?

Read It!	**Mark It!**	**Fix It!**
1 vocabulary	5 articles (ar)	1 indent
	6 nouns (n)	4 capitals
	1 pronoun (pr)	1 end mark
	5 adjectives (adj)	2 commas
	2 adverbs (adv)	1 usage
	1 <u>prepositional phrase</u>	
	4 [main clauses]	
	1 adverb clause (AC)	
	5 subject-verb pairs (s v)	
	4 openers	

finally the night, of the **annual** meeting came.

the entirely pack gathered around when it was dusk.

the summer moon was full. the air was still

Rewrite It! ____

____

____

____

____

Read It!	**Mark It!**	**Fix It!**
1 vocabulary	3 articles (ar)	4 capitals
	7 nouns (n)	3 commas
	1 pronoun (pr)	1 end mark
	1 coordinating conjunction (cc)	2 usage
	1 adverb (adv)	
	3 <u>prepositional phrases</u>	
	1 [main clause]	
	1 *who/which* clause (w/w)	
	1 adverb clause (AC)	
	3 subject-verb pairs (s v)	
	1 opener	

after the announcements, father wolf presented

mowgli who was **squatting** in the dirt as him quiet

played a game with rocks, and sticks

Rewrite It! ______________________________________

____

____

____

____

Read It!	**Mark It!**	**Fix It!**
1 vocabulary	3 articles (ar)	1 indent
	5 nouns (n)	5 capitals
	4 pronouns (pr)	2 end marks
	1 coordinating conjunction (cc)	2 commas
	2 adjectives (adj)	2 quotation marks
	2 adverbs (adv)	2 usage
	3 prepositional phrases	
	4 [main clauses]	
	1 adverb clause (AC)	
	5 subject-verb pairs (s v)	
	1 opener	

at the edge of the group shere khan paced,

and snarled while other members talked. the

man's cub is mine. give him to i now

he **threatened** vicious

Rewrite It! ____

____

____

____

____

Read It!	**Mark It!**	**Fix It!**	Day 4

Read It!

1 vocabulary

Mark It!

2 articles (ar)
4 nouns (n)
3 pronouns (pr)
4 adjectives (adj)
1 adverb (adv)
1 <u>prepositional phrase</u>
3 [main clauses]
1 *who/which* clause (w/w)
1 adverb clause (AC)
5 subject-verb pairs (s v)
1 opener

Fix It!

1 indent
3 capitals
3 commas
2 end marks
2 quotation marks
1 usage

the lone gray wolf who was named akela led the

pack because they was **considerably** strong. who

speaks, for this cub he cried out

Rewrite It! ______________________________________

____

____

____

Learn It!

Apostrophe

An **apostrophe** (') is used to indicate missing letters or ownership.

A **contraction** combines two words into one. It uses an apostrophe to show where a letter or letters have been removed. Examples of contractions are *I'm, he'll,* and *we've.*

A **possessive adjective** shows ownership and answers the question *whose.* It is formed by adding an apostrophe + *s* to a noun.

Mowgli listened to the bird's song.

> The apostrophe + *s* indicates that *bird's* is a possessive adjective. Whose song? *bird's*

Mowgli listened to the birds.

> In this sentence *birds* ends with an *s* because it is a plural noun. There is more than one bird. It would be incorrect to use an apostrophe here.

Fix It!   Insert an apostrophe to indicate that letters are missing in a contraction or to show ownership with a possessive adjective.
Remove an apostrophe if it is used incorrectly.

The animal's declared, "We'll accept the pack's ruling."

Indefinite Pronoun

An **indefinite pronoun** is not definite. It does not refer to a particular person or thing. The words below are indefinite pronouns.

Singular and Plural	Plural	Singular			
all	both		each	much	one
any	few	another	either	neither	other
more	many	anybody	everybody	nobody	somebody
most	others	anyone	everyone	no one	someone
none	own	anything	everything	nothing	something
some	several	anywhere	everywhere	nowhere	somewhere

Mark It! Write *pr* above each pronoun.

pr

Will someone speak for Mowgli?

Quotations with Attribution

When an attribution interrupts a quoted sentence, follow the established rules.

> Use commas to separate the attribution from the direct quote.

> Capitalize the first word of the quoted sentence.

> Do not capitalize the attribution unless it begins the sentence.

Commas and periods always go inside closing quotation marks.

"**W**hich of you," **t**he wolf asked, "will speak for Mowgli?"

Usage with Subject-Verb Agreement

Week 2 you learned that a personal pronoun should agree with its antecedent in number. Number means one (singular) or more than one (plural). The subject and its verb should also agree in number. If the subject is singular, the verb should be singular. If the subject is plural, the verb should be plural.

A plural noun usually ends in *s*, and a singular noun does not: one boy, two boys, five boys. However, the verb is formed in the opposite way. A singular verb usually ends in *s*, and a plural verb does not.

noun + *s* = plural noun

verb + *s* = singular verb

The boy wanders.

The singular noun *boy* (without an *s*) requires a singular verb (*wanders* with an *s*).

The boys wander.

The plural noun *boys* (with an *s*) requires a plural verb (*wander* without an *s*).

The verbs *have*, *do*, and *be* can function as either a main verb or a helping verb. Although the spelling of these verbs changes, the principle does not. Singular nouns use the verb form that ends in *s*: *has, does, is, was*. Plural nouns use the form that does not end in *s*: *have, do, are, were*.

If the subject is a singular noun, it requires a verb that ends in *s*.

The tiger is often a leader in the jungle.

The singular noun *tiger* (without an *s*) requires a singular verb (*is* ends in *s*).

The tigers are often leaders in the jungle.

The plural noun *tigers* (with an *s*) requires a plural verb (*are* does not end in *s*).

The words *who* and *which* are singular if the noun they describe is singular. The words *who* and *which* are plural if the noun they describe is plural.

Obey the law, which protects the jungle.

The *which* clause describes the singular noun *law* (without an *s*). Therefore, *which* is singular and requires a singular verb (*protects* with an *s*).

Obey the laws, which protect the jungle.

The *which* clause describes the plural noun *laws* (with an *s*). Therefore, *which* is plural and requires a plural verb (*protect* without an *s*).

Mr. Pudewa says that if you read a passage slowly out loud, your ear will usually tell you if the subject and verb do not agree.

Fix It!   Place a line through the incorrect verb and write the correct verb above it.

has *lives*

Mowgli, who ~~have~~ many brothers, ~~live~~ in a cave.

Read It!	**Mark It!**	**Fix It!**	

Read It!

1 vocabulary

Mark It!

3 articles (ar)
5 nouns (n)
4 pronouns (pr)
3 adjectives (adj)
1 adverb (adv)
2 <u>prepositional phrases</u>
4 [main clauses]
1 *who/which* clause (w/w)
5 subject-verb pairs (s v)
1 opener

Fix It!

1 indent
5 capitals
3 commas
2 quotation marks
2 end marks
2 apostrophes
2 usage

quietly, a sleepy brown bear who was named baloo

addressed the wolves. do you mean the mans cub

mowgli learn from me. ill speak for he

Rewrite It! ____

____

____

____

Read It!	**Mark It!**	**Fix It!**
1 vocabulary	3 articles (ar)	2 indents
	5 nouns (n)	2 capitals
	2 pronouns (pr)	3 commas
	1 coordinating conjunction (cc)	1 end mark
	1 adjective (adj)	2 usage
	2 adverbs (adv)	
	2 <u>prepositional phrases</u>	
	2 [main clauses]	
	1 *who/which* clause (w/w)	
	1 adverb clause (AC)	
	4 subject-verb pairs (s v)	
	2 openers	

akela asked if anyone else would **claim** he.

bagheera who was the black panther dropped

into the circle, and looked bold at the pack

Rewrite It! ____

____

____

____

____

Read It!	**Mark It!**	**Fix It!**
1 vocabulary	7 articles (ar)	2 capitals
	8 nouns (n)	1 end mark
	3 pronouns (pr)	4 commas
	1 adjective (adj)	3 quotation marks
	1 adverb (adv)	1 apostrophe
	5 prepositional phrases	2 usage
	2 [main clauses]	
	1 adverb clause (AC)	
	3 subject-verb pairs (s v)	

although im not a member of our pack he

began the laws of the jungle allows anyone in the

jungle to **purchase** the life, of a cub, for a price

No closing quotation mark because quote continues.

Rewrite It!

Read It!	**Mark It!**	**Fix It!**	Day 4
1 vocabulary	2 articles (ar)	3 capitals	
	5 nouns (n)	1 end mark	
	2 pronouns (pr)	2 commas	
	4 adjectives (adj)	1 quotation marks	
	2 <u>prepositional phrases</u>	1 apostrophe	
	3 [main clauses]	3 usage	
	1 *who/which* clause (w/w)		
	4 subject-verb pairs (s v)		

No opening quotation mark because quote continues.

this cub who live with the pack is innocently.

ive killed a fat bull. take them as payment

to **preserve** his life

Rewrite It! ____

____

____

____

Learn It!

That Clause

A ***that* clause** is a dependent clause that begins with the word *that* and contains a subject and a verb. Because *that* clauses are essential to the sentence, they do not take commas.

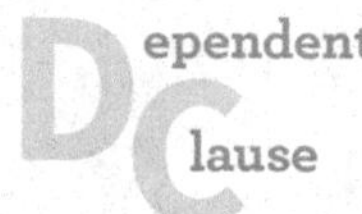

Comma

 *That* clauses do not take commas.

Mark It! Place parentheses around the *that* clause and write ***that*** above the word *that*. Write *v* above each verb and *s* above each subject.

         that   s   v

He learned **(**that the jungle pools were cool**)**.

Demonstrative Pronoun

A **demonstrative pronoun** points to a particular person or thing. There are only four demonstrative pronouns: *this, that, these, those.*

Think About It!

A word can perform only one part of speech at a time. Indefinite, demonstrative, and possessive pronouns function as adjectives when they come before a noun. When they do not come before a noun, they function as pronouns.

Adjective: Mother Wolf declared that Mowgli was her cub.

> *Her* is an adjective because it comes before a noun and tells whose cub.

Pronoun: Mother Wolf declared that Mowgli was hers.

> *Hers* is possessive pronoun that follows the linking verb. A noun does not follow the word *hers*.

Adjective: Some animals asked questions.

> In this sentence *Some* is an adjective because it comes before a noun and tells which animals asked questions.

Pronoun: Some asked questions.

> In this sentence *Some* is an indefinite pronoun that functions as the subject of the clause. A noun does not directly follow the word.

Adjective: That boy lived in the jungle.

> In this sentence *That* is an adjective because it comes before a noun and tells which boy.

Pronoun: That was a tragic event.

> In this sentence *That* is a demonstrative pronoun that functions as the subject of the clause. A noun does not directly follow the word.

That Clause: Mother Wolf knew (that the human child needed help).

> In this sentence *that* begins a dependent clause, which means it follows the pattern that + subject + verb and does not express a complete thought.

That Clause

Pattern:
that + subject + verb

First Word:
that

Commas:
none

Marking:
that

Usage with Verb Tense

Verb tense indicates when an action occurs: present, past, or future.

Week 6 you learned that a common mistake in writing is mixing singular subjects with plural verbs and vice versa. Another writing mistake is mixing verb tenses. A passage should not unexpectedly switch tenses from past to present or from present to future.

Present tense indicates an action that happens right now or regularly. Form a present tense verb by using the basic verb (hunt, swim) or the verb + *s* (hunts, swims).

Wolves hunt daily.

> *Hunt* is a present tense verb. It does not end in s because the subject *wolves* is plural.

Mowgli swims daily.

> *Swims* is a present tense verb. It ends in *s* because the subject *Mowgli* is singular.

The jungle is a thick tropical forest.

> *Is* is also a present tense verb. The verbs *be*, *have*, and *do* are irregular.
> Thus, it is best to memorize their present forms: *am, is, are, has, have, does, do.*

Past tense indicates an action that occurred in the past. Form a past tense verb by adding *-ed* to a verb (hunted) or using an irregular verb form (swam).

Wolves hunted before dawn.

> *Hunted* is a past tense verb. Like many verbs it forms the past tense by adding *-ed.*

Mowgli swam before dawn.

> *Swam* is a past tense verb. Irregular verbs form the past tense in an unpredictable way. The past tense of *swim* is not *swimmed* but *swam*. To spell past tense verbs correctly, consult a dictionary, which lists all forms of the verb. In other words, if you look up "swim" in the dictionary, it will instruct you to use "swam" in the past tense.

The jungle was a thick tropical forest.

> *Was* is also a past tense verb. The verbs *be*, *have*, and *do* are irregular. It is best to memorize their past forms: *was, were, had, did.*

The story *Mowgli and Shere Khan* has already happened, so the narrated part of the story is told in the past tense. In dialogue, however, the exact words that a character said are provided. Therefore, the tense in quoted sentences may change depending on whether the character refers to a past, present, or future event.

Fix It!   Place a line through the incorrect verb and write the correct verb above it.

Bagheera ~~offers~~ **offered** the bull. "Yesterday I ~~kill~~ **killed** it. Today it ~~paid~~ **pays**

for the cub's life."

Present Tense

verb
verb + s

includes
am, is, are
has, have
does, do

Past Tense

verb + ed
irregular form

includes
was, were
had
did

Read It!	**Mark It!**	**Fix It!**	
			Day 1

Read It!	**Mark It!**	**Fix It!**
1 vocabulary	4 articles (ar)	1 indent
	4 nouns (n)	4 capitals
	4 pronouns (pr)	4 commas
	1 coordinating conjunction (cc)	2 quotation marks
	6 adjectives (adj)	2 end marks
	1 adverb (adv)	2 apostrophes
	2 <u>prepositional phrases</u>	3 usage
	4 [main clauses]	
	1 *that* clause (that)	
	5 subject-verb pairs (s v)	
	2 openers	

the packs only interest were, that you were

given a free meal. **eagerly**, they cry who cares

hell die in the chilly winter rains, or scorch

in the summer sun

Rewrite It! ____

____

____

____

Read It!	**Mark It!**	**Fix It!**
1 vocabulary	2 articles (ar)	1 indent
	4 nouns (n)	3 capitals
	2 pronouns (pr)	3 commas
	4 adjectives (adj)	1 end mark
	3 adverbs (adv)	3 usage
	2 <u>prepositional phrases</u>	
	1 [main clause]	
	1 *who/which* clause (w/w)	
	1 adverb clause (AC)	
	1 *that* clause (that)	
	4 subject-verb pairs (s v)	

as he withdrew from the pack, shere khan

who mutters **thickly** under his breath is disappointed,

that the ugly human creature is still not his

Rewrite It! ____

____

____

____

____

Read It!	**Mark It!**	**Fix It!**	

1 vocabulary	3 articles (ar)	1 indent
	7 nouns (n)	3 capitals
	1 pronoun (pr)	3 commas
	1 coordinating conjunction (cc)	1 end mark
	6 adjectives (adj)	3 apostrophes
	3 prepositional phrases	1 number
	2 [main clauses]	2 usage
	2 subject-verb pairs (s v)	
	2 openers	

for the next 10 years mowgli learns the way's,

of the jungle. before long his could **detect** every

birds note, and every animals track

Rewrite It!

Read It!	**Mark It!**	**Fix It!**	Day 4

Read It!	Mark It!	Fix It!
1 vocabulary	1 article (ar)	3 capitals
	5 nouns (n)	3 commas
	2 pronouns (pr)	1 end mark
	1 coordinating conjunction (cc)	1 apostrophe
	4 adjectives (adj)	2 usage
	1 adverb (adv)	
	3 prepositional phrases	
	2 [main clauses]	
	1 adverb clause (AC)	
	3 subject-verb pairs (s v)	
	2 openers	

baloo taught him to climb, for honey. in his **leisure**,

mowgli happily swims in the jungles pools when

they felt dirty, or hot

Rewrite It! ____

____

____

____

Learn It!

Run-On

A **run-on** occurs when a sentence has main clauses that are not connected properly.
There are two types of run-ons: fused sentence and comma splice.

A **fused sentence** is two main clauses placed in one sentence without any
punctuation between them.

A **comma splice** is two main clauses placed in one sentence with only a comma
between them.

The easiest way to fix a run-on is to place a period at the end of each main clause.

Find It!   Look for two main clauses that have no punctuation or only a comma
between them.

Fix It!   Correct a run-on by putting a period between the main clauses.
Capitalize the first word of the new sentence.

[Mowgli swam in the pools]. [he climbed for honey].

smoothly [he swung in the trees].

Fused sentence:
MC MC

Comma Splice:
MC, MC

These patterns are
always wrong!

Fix:
MC. MC.

Reflexive Pronoun Usage

Week 1 you learned that a **reflexive pronoun** ends in -self (singular) or -selves (plural) and
refers to the subject of the same sentence.

This means that a reflexive pronoun is never a subject. It also means that a reflexive
pronoun is used when the pronoun following the verb refers to the subject.

Fix It!   Place a line through the incorrect pronoun and write the correct
pronoun above it.

I

"My friend and ~~myself~~ swam in the pool," said Baloo.

himself

Mowgli taught ~~him~~ how to swing on the vines. The pool

him

cooled ~~himself~~.

Apostrophe with Possessive Adjectives

Week 6 you learned that a **possessive adjective** shows ownership and answers the question *whose*. A singular possessive adjective is formed by adding an apostrophe + *s* to a noun. However, a plural possessive adjective is formed differently.

Mowgli listened to the bird's song.

> *Bird's* is a singular possessive adjective. The apostrophe + *s* indicates that Mowgli listened to the song belonging to one bird. Whose song? *bird's*

Mowgli listened to the birds' songs.

> *Birds'* is a plural possessive adjective. The apostrophe after the *s* indicates that Mowgli listened to the songs belonging to more than one bird. Whose songs? *birds'*

To form singular possessives

> Write the singular form of the noun: tiger, man.
>
> Add an apostrophe + *s*: tiger's, man's.

To form plural possessives

> Write the plural form of the noun: tigers, men.
>
> If the plural noun ends in *s*, add an apostrophe after the *s*: tigers'.
>
> If the plural noun does not end in *s*, add an apostrophe + *s*: men's.

> *Fix It!* Insert an apostrophe to form a possessive adjective.
> Remove an apostrophe when a noun is plural, not possessive.

adj   *adj*

The men's needs often conflicted with the beasts' needs

adj

or even the jungle's needs.

Apostrophes are used with possessive adjectives, never plural nouns.

Read It! **Mark It!** **Fix It!**

1 vocabulary

2 articles (ar) 3 capitals
6 nouns (n) 4 commas
3 pronouns (pr) 2 end marks
1 coordinating conjunction (cc) 1 apostrophe
2 adjectives (adj) 2 usage
1 adverb (adv)
5 <u>prepositional phrases</u>
2 [main clauses]
1 *who/which* clause (w/w)
3 subject-verb pairs (s v)
2 openers

in fear, mowgli **awkwardly** holds the trees branches

which spread in all directions with practice he

swung, and flung him through them, like a monkey

Rewrite It! ____

____

____

____

Read It!	**Mark It!**	**Fix It!**	

Read It!	Mark It!	Fix It!
1 vocabulary	2 articles (ar)	1 indent
	3 nouns (n)	3 capitals
	4 pronouns (pr)	3 commas
	1 coordinating conjunction (cc)	3 end marks
	6 adjectives (adj)	1 apostrophe
	1 adverb (adv)	3 usage
	2 prepositional phrases	
	3 [main clauses]	
	1 adverb clause (AC)	
	4 subject-verb pairs (s v)	
	2 openers	

as he learned the ways of the jungle, himself

grew tough he is happy, and **carefree**, he only

worries, about his stomachs next meal

Rewrite It! ____

____

____

____

____

Read It!	**Mark It!**	**Fix It!**
1 vocabulary	1 article (ar)	3 capitals
	6 nouns (n)	1 comma
	3 pronouns (pr)	2 end marks
	2 adjectives (adj)	1 apostrophe
	1 adverb (adv)	3 usage
	3 <u>prepositional phrases</u>	
	2 [main clauses]	
	1 adverb clause (AC)	
	1 *that* clause (that)	
	4 subject-verb pairs (s v)	
	2 openers	

he discovered, that the wolves would drop their **gaze**

if he stared direct at your eye's for fun mowgli does

it on purpose

Rewrite It! ____

____

____

____

Read It!	**Mark It!**	**Fix It!**	
			Day 4

Read It!	**Mark It!**	**Fix It!**
1 vocabulary	4 nouns (n)	2 capitals
	2 pronouns (pr)	3 commas
	5 adjectives (adj)	2 apostrophes
	2 <u>prepositional phrases</u>	2 end marks
	2 [main clauses]	1 usage
	2 subject-verb pairs (s v)	
	2 openers	

on other **occasions**, he would pull thorn's, from his

friends sore paws, this eased his suffering

Rewrite It! ____

____

____

____

____

Learn It!

Interjection

An **interjection** expresses an emotion. When it expresses a strong emotion, use an exclamation mark and capitalize the word that follows. When it does not express a strong emotion, use a comma.

Mark It!   Write *int* above each interjection.

Fix It!   Place a comma or an exclamation mark after each interjection. Place three short lines below letters that should be capitalized.

int
Grr! the man's cub is mine!

int
Oh, we'll see about that.

Run-On

Week 8 you learned that a run-on occurs when a sentence has main clauses that are not connected properly. There are two types of run-ons: fused sentence and comma splice.

Mowgli grew in stature, Shere Khan waited.

This is a comma splice. It is grammatically wrong because the two main clauses are separated with only a comma.

Mowgli grew in stature. Shere Khan waited.

The easiest way to fix a run-on is to place a period at the end of each main clause.

Mowgli grew in stature, **and** Shere Khan waited.

Another way to fix a run-on is to connect the clauses with a comma and a coordinating conjunction. Use this option when the content of the main clauses fits well in the same sentence.

Mowgli grew in stature and Shere Khan waited.

This is grammatically wrong. If you connect two main clauses with a coordinating conjunction, you must place a comma before the coordinating conjunction.

Comma

, Use a comma before a coordinating conjunction when it connects two main clauses. **PATTERN MC, cc MC**

Mark It!   Write *cc* above each coordinating conjunction.

Fix It!   Add a comma before a *cc* that connects two main clauses.

    S   V   CC   S   V
[Shere Khan fed the cubs], but [he also mocked them].

Parts of Speech (8)

Interjection
Definition:

An interjection expresses an emotion.

Fused sentence:

MC MC

Comma Splice:

MC, MC

These patterns are always wrong!

Fix:

MC. MC.

Fix:

MC, cc MC.

Usage with Subject-Verb Agreement

Week 6 you learned that the subject and its verb should agree in number. If the subject noun is singular, the verb should be singular. If the subject noun is plural, the verb should be plural.

When a pronoun is the subject of a clause, only the third-person singular uses a verb form that ends in *s*. The main thing to remember is this: if the subject is a singular noun or the pronoun *he*, *she*, *it*, the verb should end in *s*.

The chart provides an example of this with three verbs: *wander, run, do*.

Like singular nouns, the pronouns *he, she, it* require a verb that ends in *s*.

2 numbers	3 persons	Subjective		
singular	1st	I wander.	I run.	I do.
	2nd	You wander.	You run.	You do.
	3rd	He, she, it wanders.	He, she, it runs.	He, she, it does.
plural	1st	We wander.	We run.	We do.
	2nd	You wander.	You run.	You do.
	3rd	They wander.	They run.	They do.

Interrogative Adverb

An **interrogative adverb** is an adverb used to begin a question. The interrogative adverbs are *how, when, where,* and *why*. When these words begin a question, they function as adverbs.

Mark It!   Write *adv* above each adverb.

adv   *adv*
Why do bees sting, Baloo? How will you collect the honey?

Think About It!

Questions, also known as interrogative sentences, are often written in a strange word order. As a result, marking them can be difficult. With a question, it is easier to determine parts of speech if you first make the question into a statement.

Question: Do bees sting?

Statement: Bees do sting.

In a question, the subject separates the helping verb and action verb. In a statement, the helping verb is next to the action verb, making it easier to identify the complete verb phrase.

Question: Were the wolves always hungry?

Statement: The wolves were always hungry.

In a question, the verb comes before the subject. In a statement, the sentence is placed in standard subject-verb order, making it easier to identify that *hungry* is an adjective because it follows a linking verb and describes the subject (wolves).

Read It!	**Mark It!**	**Fix It!**
1 vocabulary	2 articles (ar)	1 indent
	6 nouns (n)	1 capital
	2 pronouns (pr)	2 commas
	1 coordinating conjunction (cc)	1 end mark
	2 adjectives (adj)	2 apostrophes
	1 adverb (adv)	
	2 <u>prepositional phrases</u>	
	2 [main clauses]	
	1 adverb clause (AC)	
	3 subject-verb pairs (s v)	
	1 opener	

mowgli would watch the villagers huts in the

evenings but he **mistrusted** people because

they cruelly set traps, for his friend's

Rewrite It! ____

____

____

____

Read It!	**Mark It!**	**Fix It!**	Day 2
1 vocabulary	1 article (ar)	1 indent	
	7 nouns (n)	6 capitals	
	1 pronoun (pr)	4 commas	
	1 coordinating conjunction (cc)	2 end marks	
	2 adjectives (adj)	1 usage	
	1 adverb (adv)		
	1 <u>prepositional phrase</u>		
	3 [main clauses]		
	1 *who/which* clause (w/w)		
	1 adverb clause (AC)		
	5 subject-verb pairs (s v)		
	2 openers		

akela aged and shere khan waited, **craftily**

shere khan who rewarded his followers feeds scraps

to the younger wolves because they wanted food

Rewrite It! ____

____

____

____

Read It! | **Mark It!** | **Fix It!**

1 vocabulary	1 article (ar)	1 indent
	5 nouns (n)	4 capitals
	2 pronouns (pr)	4 commas
	5 adjectives (adj)	2 quotation marks
	2 adverbs (adv)	1 end mark
	3 prepositional phrases	2 apostrophes
	1 coordinating conjunction (cc)	1 number
	2 [main clauses]	3 usage
	1 *that* clause (that)	
	3 subject-verb pairs (s v)	
	1 opener	

at times, shere khan would ask why is such

impressively hunter's as yourselves **content**,

that you is led by 1 dying wolf, and a mans cub

Rewrite It! ____

____

____

____

Read It!	**Mark It!**	**Fix It!**	Day 4
1 vocabulary	1 article (ar)	5 capitals	
	3 nouns (n)	4 commas	
	2 pronouns (pr)	2 quotation marks	
	4 adjectives (adj)	2 end marks	
	1 adverb (adv)	2 apostrophes	
	1 interjection (int)	3 usage	
	1 <u>prepositional phrase</u>		
	3 [main clauses]		
	1 *who/which* clause (w/w)		
	4 subject-verb pairs (s v)		
	2 openers		

at other time's, himself would comment hah

you fears mowglis eyes. angrily the young

wolves who feel **embarrassed** would grumble

Rewrite It! ____

____

____

____

____

Learn It!

Coordinating Conjunction

A **coordinating conjunction** (for, and, nor, but, or, yet, so) connects the same type of words, phrases, or clauses.

FANBOYS

You have learned three comma rules to use when a sentence has a coordinating conjunction. In this lesson you will learn the fourth rule.

Shere Khan fed the cubs leftovers, scraps, and bones.

a, b, and c

In this sentence the coordinating conjunction *and* connects three nouns: *leftovers, scraps,* and *bones.* Two commas are used.

The cubs were noisy and hungry.

a and b

In this sentence the coordinating conjunction *and* connects two adjectives: *noisy* and *hungry.* No comma is used.

Shere Khan fed the cubs, but he also mocked them.

MC, cc MC

In this sentence the coordinating conjunction *but* connects two main clauses. A subject and verb pair (Shere Khan fed) comes before the coordinating conjunction, and a subject and verb pair (he mocked) comes after. When a subject and verb pair follows the coordinating conjunction, use a comma.

Compare the last sentence to this sentence:

Shere Khan fed the cubs but also mocked them.

MC cc 2nd verb

In this sentence the coordinating conjunction *but* connects two verbs: *fed* but *mocked.* A subject and verb (Shere Khan fed) come before the coordinating conjunction, but only a verb (mocked) comes after. When only a verb follows the coordinating conjunction, do not use a comma. The verbs have the same subject. This is the same pattern as **a and b** when *a* and *b* are verbs.

Comma

 Do not use a comma before a coordinating conjunction when it connects two verbs.
PATTERN MC cc 2nd verb

 Use a comma before a coordinating conjunction when it connects two main clauses.
PATTERN MC, cc MC

Mark It!   Write *cc* above each coordinating conjunction.

Fix It!   Remove a comma before a *cc* that connects two verbs.
Add a comma before a *cc* that connects two main clauses.

<pre>
    S   V   cc   V
[Mowgli knew of Shere Khan's hatred, but was not afraid].

      S   V   cc   S   V
[Shere Khan hated Mowgli], but [Mowgli was not afraid].
</pre>

#6 Vss Opener

A **#6 vss opener** is a very short sentence.

Very short means two to five words. *Sentence* means it must have a main clause.

Shere Khan roared.

This sentence is short because it has three words.
It is a sentence because it has a main clause. It is a #6 vss opener.

Mark It!   Write ⑥ above the first word of a very short sentence.

⑥
    S   V

[Mowgli ignored him].

Noun of Direct Address

A **noun of direct address** (NDA) is a noun used to refer to someone directly. It names the person spoken to.

It can appear at any natural pause in a quoted sentence.

"Mowgli, if you are wise, you will fear him," Bagheera said.

"If you are wise, Mowgli, you will fear him," Bagheera said.

"If you are wise, you will fear him, Mowgli," Bagheera said.

Because a noun can perform only one function in a sentence, a noun of direct address is never the subject of the sentence. In these sentences the noun of direct address is *Mowgli* because this is the noun used to address Mowgli directly. The subject of the main clause is *you*.

Comma

Place commas around a noun of direct address.

Fix It!   Add commas to separate the noun of direct address from the sentence.

"Mowgli, Shere Khan is dangerous," Bagheera warned.

Do not include the NDA in the main clause square brackets. This will help you remember that the NDA is not the subject of the sentence.

           S   V   V

"Mowgli, [you will fear him].

Read It!	**Mark It!**	**Fix It!**

Read It!	Mark It!	Fix It!
1 vocabulary	5 nouns (n)	1 indent
	5 pronouns (pr)	7 capitals
	2 coordinating conjunctions (cc)	4 commas
	4 adverbs (adv)	2 quotation marks
	3 [main clauses]	2 end marks
	1 *who/which* clause (w/w)	2 usage
	4 subject-verb pairs (s v)	
	1 opener	

urgently, bagheera who had eyes and ears everywhere warned mowgli. shere khan hate you, and plan to harm you how often have i told you this

Rewrite It! ____

____

____

____

Read It!	**Mark It!**	**Fix It!**	Day 2
1 vocabulary	4 nouns (n)	1 indent	
	5 pronouns (pr)	6 capitals	
	2 coordinating conjunctions (cc)	4 commas	
	1 adjective (adj)	2 quotation marks	
	2 adverbs (adv)	4 end marks	
	1 interjection (int)	3 apostrophes	
	1 <u>prepositional phrase</u>	1 number	
	4 [main clauses]	2 usage	
	4 subject-verb pairs (s v)		
	1 opener		

mowgli **shrugged** pooh youve told myself

and ive heard you 100s of times, i is not

scared, and wont hide bagheera

Rewrite It! ____

____

____

____

Read It!	**Mark It!**	**Fix It!**	Day 3

Read It!

1 vocabulary

Mark It!

2 articles (ar)
6 nouns (n)
2 pronouns (pr)
1 coordinating conjunction (cc)
3 adjectives (adj)
1 adverb (adv)
1 prepositional phrase
2 [main clauses]
1 adverb clause (AC)
1 *that* clause (that)
4 subject-verb pairs (s v)

Fix It!

1 indent
5 capitals
4 commas
2 quotation marks
2 end marks
1 apostrophe
1 usage

you should be **concerned** because youre

in danger mowgli baloo the pack and even the

silly deer knows, that shere khan is hateful

Rewrite It! ______________________________

____

____

____

Read It!	**Mark It!**	**Fix It!**
1 vocabulary	2 articles (ar)	1 indent
	6 nouns (n)	3 capitals
	1 pronoun (pr)	3 commas
	1 coordinating conjunction (cc)	1 end mark
	3 adjectives (adj)	1 apostrophe
	1 adverb (adv)	3 usage
	1 <u>prepositional phrase</u>	
	1 [main clause]	
	2 *that* clauses (that)	
	3 subject-verb pairs (s v)	
	1 opener	

bagheera argued that shere khan selfishly

manipulates the younger wolves, and tells it,

that mens cubs had no place, in the pack

Rewrite It! ____

____

____

____

____

Learn It!

Mark It!

You no longer need to label articles, nouns, pronouns, adjectives, adverbs, and interjections. However, you will continue to label coordinating conjunctions and subject-verb pairs, underline prepositional phrases, and mark clauses. Recognizing the basic clause and phrase structure of a sentence will help you punctuate sentences properly.

Adverb Clause

An **adverb clause** is a dependent clause that begins with a www word and contains a subject and a verb.

Week 5 you began looking for www words and marking adverb clauses. A www word is called a subordinating conjunction. The acronym *www.asia.b* reminds you of the eight most common subordinating conjunctions. However, these are not the only words that begin an adverb clause. Other words can function as www words too.

Memorize It!   **when   while   where   as   since   if   although   because
after   before   until   unless   whenever   whereas   than**

A www word must have a subject and verb after it to begin an adverb clause.

#5 Clausal Opener

A **#5 clausal opener** is a sentence that begins with an adverb clause.

The #5 clausal opener will always have a comma and a main clause after it.

Mark It!   Write ⑤ above the first word of a sentence that starts with an adverb clause.

⑤
AC   S   V
(Whenever Mowgli could), he helped the pack.

Comma

Use a comma after an adverb clause that comes before a main clause.
PATTERN AC, MC

Do not use a comma before an adverb clause.
PATTERN MC AC

Fix It!   Add a comma after an adverb clause.
Remove a comma before an adverb clause.

AC   S   V   V   S   V   V
(Because Akela was aging), [he could not control Shere Khan].

            S   V   AC   S   V
[Mowgli helped the pack], (whenever he could).

Adverb Clause

Pattern:
www word +
subject + verb

First Word:
www word

Commas:
after, not before

Marking:
AC

Verb Phrase

A **verb phrase** is one main verb (action or linking) and one or more helping verbs. Review the helping verbs.

The wolves should have been hunting that fall.

> The words *should have been hunting* form the verb of the sentence. Since more than one word is used to form the verb, the group of words is called a verb phrase.

> Sometimes people write or say *The wolves should of been hunting. Could of, should of, would of* are incorrect. *Of* is not a helping verb. Use *have* instead of *of*.

Usage with Verb Tense

Verb tense indicates when an action occurs: present, past, or future.

When helping verbs are used, the helping verb, *not the main verb*, indicates verb tense.

Week 7 you learned that verb tense must remain consistent and accurate. A passage should not unexpectedly switch tenses from past to present or from present to future. Although distinguishing between the simple present and simple past is not particularly difficult, verb tense can be more difficult when forms of the verbs *be* and *have* are included in a verb phrase.

Present tense indicates an action that happens right now or regularly. A present tense verb phrase can include helping verbs *am, is, are, has, have*.

Present Tense helping verbs include *am, is, are, has, have*.

> Mowgli *is swimming* right now.
>> Wolves *are hunting* right now.
> Mowgli *has been swimming* since morning.
>> Wolves *have been hunting* since morning.
> Mowgli *has swum* near the village.
>> Wolves *have hunted* near the village.

Past tense indicates an action that occurred in the past. A past tense verb phrase can include helping verbs *was, were, had*.

Past Tense helping verbs include *was, were, had*.

> Mowgli *was swimming* when Shere Khan roared.
>> Wolves *were hunting* when Shere Khan roared.
> Mowgli *had been swimming* before the meeting began.
>> Wolves *had been hunting* before the meeting began.
> Mowgli *had swum* alone once before.
>> Wolves *had hunted* man once before.

Verb usage is affected not only by tense, but also by number. In the examples above the singular subject *Mowgli* uses the helping verbs *is, has,* and *was*. They end in *s*. The plural subject *wolves* uses the helping verbs *are, have,* and *were*. They do not end in *s*.

Hunt is a regular verb. It forms the past tense and past participle by adding *-ed*. *Swam* is an irregular verb. It forms the past tense and past participle in an unpredictable way. The past tense of *swim* is not *swimmed* but *swam*, and when combined with a form of *have*, it is *swum*. To spell past tense verbs correctly, consult a dictionary, which lists all forms of the verb.

Read It!	**Mark It!**	**Fix It!**	
1 vocabulary	1 <u>prepositional phrase</u>	5 capitals	
	1 [main clause]	2 commas	
	2 adverb clauses (AC)	1 end mark	
	3 subject-verb pairs (s v)	1 apostrophe	
	1 opener	2 usage	

although shere khan would not kill mowgli in

the jungle akela was simple too old to control the

tigers response, whenever he becomes **aggressive**

Rewrite It! ____

____

____

____

Read It!	**Mark It!**	**Fix It!**
1 vocabulary	2 <u>prepositional phrases</u>	1 indent
	1 coordinating conjunction (cc)	7 capitals
	1 adverb clause (AC)	4 commas
	4 [main clauses]	2 quotation marks
	5 subject-verb pairs (s v)	2 end marks
	1 opener	1 apostrophe
		1 number
		2 usage

as bagheera paced he **hesitated**, and said

in 2 years time you will be a grown man mowgli.

shere khan had taught the wolves they listens to him

Rewrite It! ____

____

____

____

____

Read It!	**Mark It!**	**Fix It!**
1 vocabulary	1 coordinating conjunction (cc)	1 indent
	2 <u>prepositional phrases</u>	4 capitals
	3 [main clauses]	2 commas
	3 subject-verb pairs (s v)	4 quotation marks
		3 end marks
		2 apostrophes
		2 usage

shouldnt a man run, with his brother's mowgli

reasoned truly, i had obeyed the laws of the jungle,

and had helped the pack

Rewrite It! _______________________________

____

____

____

____

Read It!	**Mark It!**	**Fix It!**	Day 4
1 vocabulary	2 <u>prepositional phrases</u>	1 indent	
	3 [main clauses]	4 capitals	
	2 *who/which* clauses (w/w)	5 commas	
	1 *that* clause (that)	2 quotation marks	
	1 adverb clause (AC)	2 end marks	
	7 subject-verb pairs (s v)	1 apostrophe	
	2 openers	2 usage	

bagheera who stretched him shut his eye's. since

mowgli was **oblivious** to their hatred he decided,

that he should share his secret mowgli feel

under my jaw, which reveal my secrets

Rewrite It! ____

____

____

____

Review It!

Clause

A **clause** is a group of related words that contains both a subject and a verb.

Recognizing the basic clause and phrase structure of a sentence will help you punctuate sentences properly. Label the subject-verb pairs to determine how many clauses are in each sentence. Focus on the word that begins the clause to determine if it is a dependent clause or a main clause. After you have identified each clause, check its placement in the sentence and follow the comma rules.

Main Clause

A **main clause** expresses a complete thought, so it can stand alone as a sentence.

[Bagheera rescued Mowgli].

    Every sentence must have a main clause.

[Bagheera rescued Mowgli], and [this angered Shere Khan].

    Two main clauses can be placed in the same sentence if they are connected with a comma and a coordinating conjunction. **MC, cc MC**

MC
Main Clause

Contains:
subject + verb

stands alone

Dependent Clause

A **dependent clause** does not express a complete thought, so it cannot stand alone as a sentence.

In this book you have learned three types of dependent clauses.

Who/Which Clause

[Bagheera, (who sympathized with Mowgli), rescued him].

    begins with *who* or *which* (a relative pronoun)
    uses commas unless essential

That Clause

[Bagheera told Mowgli] (that he had been born in captivity).

    begins with *that* (a relative pronoun)
    does not use commas

Adverb Clause

(Although Mowgli was a boy), [he lived with wolves].

[Bagheera rescued Mowgli] (when he spoke at Council Rock).

    begins with a www word (a subordinating conjunction)
    uses a comma after but not before (**AC, MC** but **MC AC**)

Dependent
Clause

Contains:
subject + verb

cannot stand alone

Dependent Clause

A **dependent clause** begins with a word that causes it to be an incomplete thought. Therefore, a dependent clause must be added to a main clause.

Read and decide which kind of dependent clause is in each sentence.

Circle the correct answer.

Insert commas where needed.

Shere Khan who desired to rule ignored the laws of the jungle.

who/which　　　　*that*　　　　AC before MC　　　　AC after MC

Mowgli did not realize that Shere Khan hated him.

who/which　　　　*that*　　　　AC before MC　　　　AC after MC

Since the wolves accepted him Mowgli ignored the tiger's threat.

who/which　　　　*that*　　　　AC before MC　　　　AC after MC

Mowgli could tell a fish by its splash when it leaped in the water.

who/which　　　　*that*　　　　AC before MC　　　　AC after MC

The first word of a clause usually indicates the type of clause. However, accurate identification requires one to consider the way the entire clause functions in the sentence.

Who desired to rule the jungle?

This is a main clause. It expresses a complete thought. *Who* is an interrogative pronoun asking a question. It does not begin a *who/which* clause.

That boy grew up with wolves.

This is a main clause. It expresses a complete thought. *That* is an adjective describing the word *boy*.

Read It!

1 vocabulary

Mark It!

1 coordinating conjunction (cc)
3 <u>prepositional phrases</u>
2 [main clauses]
2 subject-verb pairs (s v)
2 openers

Fix It!

1 indent
3 capitals
2 commas
2 end marks
2 apostrophes
1 usage

under his chin, bagheeras muscle's was hidden,

beneath his black hair mowgli felt a small **jagged**

spot and wondered about it

Rewrite It! _______________________________________

____

____

____

____

Read It!	**Mark It!**	**Fix It!**	Day 2
1 vocabulary	1 coordinating conjunction (cc)	2 capitals	
	3 <u>prepositional phrases</u>	3 commas	
	2 [main clauses]	2 end marks	
	2 *that* clauses (that)	1 apostrophe	
	4 subject-verb pairs (s v)	1 usage	
	2 openers		

bagheera confessed, that nobody in the jungle knows

that he **bore** the mark of the chain, that spot was it's

sign, and would be with him forever

Rewrite It! ____

____

____

____

Read It!   **Mark It!**   **Fix It!**

Read It!	Mark It!	Fix It!
1 vocabulary	3 <u>prepositional phrases</u>	3 capitals
	2 [main clauses]	3 commas
	1 *who/which* clause (w/w)	2 end marks
	1 *that* clause (that)	1 apostrophe
	1 adverb clause (AC)	1 usage
	5 subject-verb pairs (s v)	
	2 openers	

because he was born in **captivity** he had never lived

in the jungle which should of been his home that was

the reason, that hed paid for mowgli to join the pack

Rewrite It! ____

____

____

____

Read It!	**Mark It!**	**Fix It!**	Day 4
1 vocabulary	1 coordinating conjunction (cc)	1 indent	
	2 <u>prepositional phrases</u>	3 capitals	
	3 [main clauses]	4 commas	
	1 *that* clause (that)	2 quotation marks	
	1 adverb clause (AC)	2 end marks	
	5 subject-verb pairs (s v)	2 apostrophes	
	1 opener	1 usage	

bagheera explained **miserably** my mother

died in the kings palace, in that place, men fed

the captive's and I until I finally understood, that

I was stronger than man

Rewrite It! ____

____

____

____

Learn It!

#4 -ing Opener

A **#4 -ing opener** is a sentence that begins with a participial phrase. The first word in the sentence must be a word that ends with an -ing suffix.

Wanting to understand, Mowgli searched Bagheera's eyes.

A #4 -ing opener begins with a verb form that ends in -ing. This is a called a participle. That means *wanting* is not a verb. An -ing phrase usually includes additional words like adverbs, nouns, infinitives, prepositional phrases, or dependent clauses. The entire phrase *wanting to understand* describes Mowgli. The entire phrase is called a participial phrase (-ing opener) and functions as an adjective.

Wanting to understand**,** Mowgli searched Bagheera's eyes.

A comma separates the -ing opener from the main clause.

Wanting to understand, **[**Mowgli searched Bagheera's eyes**]**.

A main clause follows the comma. If you remove the -ing opener, a sentence will remain.

Wanting to understand, **Mowgli** searched Bagheera's eyes.

The thing after the comma must be the thing doing the inging. *Mowgli* is the thing (subject of main clause) after the comma. *Mowgli* is doing the *wanting*.

Memorize It!   **-ing word/phrase, main clause**

Comma

Use a comma after an -ing opener, even if it is short.
PATTERN -ing word/phrase, main clause

Mark It!   Write ④ above the first word of a sentence that starts with an -ing opener.

Fix It!   Add a comma to separate the -ing opener from the main clause.

④
                        s   v
Breaking the lock**, [**Bagheera bounded away**]**.

Think About It!

Many words end with the letters *ing*. However, only a verb form that has the letters -ing added to the word can be used to begin a #4 -ing opener.

Morning begins at the break of day.

Nouns like *king, sibling, morning,* and *duckling* can never begin a #4 opener. *Morning* is a noun that ends in *ing.*

During the night wolves howled.

The prepositions *concerning, according to, regarding,* and *during* can begin a #2 prepositional opener but never a #4 -ing opener. *During* is a preposition that ends in *ing.*

Read It!	**Mark It!**	**Fix It!**	

Read It! **Mark It!** **Fix It!** Day 1

1 vocabulary

3 <u>prepositional phrases</u>

1 [main clause]

1 *that* clause (that)

1 adverb clause (AC)

3 subject-verb pairs (s v)

1 opener

2 capitals

3 commas

1 end mark

2 apostrophes

1 number

2 usage

breaking the lock with 1 **blow** of his paw bagheera had

escapes from the palace, when he realized, that the

chain's couldnt hold himself

Rewrite It!

Read It!	**Mark It!**	**Fix It!**	Day 2
1 vocabulary	1 <u>prepositional phrase</u>	4 capitals	
	1 coordinating conjunction (cc)	4 commas	
	3 [main clauses]	2 quotation marks	
	1 *that* clause (that)	2 end marks	
	4 subject-verb pairs (s v)	1 apostrophe	
	1 opener	1 usage	

hoping **cautiously**, that mowgli would understand

bagheera made his point mowgli you must return

to our people or youll be killed

Rewrite It! ____

____

____

____

Read It!	**Mark It!**	**Fix It!**
1 vocabulary	1 <u>prepositional phrase</u>	1 indent
	3 [main clauses]	5 capitals
	1 *that* clause (that)	3 commas
	4 subject-verb pairs (s v)	2 quotation marks
	1 opener	2 end marks
		1 apostrophe
		2 usage

pacing in **distress** mowgli replies youre

confusing me, what has i done that anyone

would want to kill me

Rewrite It! ________________________________

____

____

____

Read It!	Mark It!	Fix It!	
1 vocabulary	1 coordinating conjunction (cc)	2 indents	
	3 <u>prepositional phrases</u>	5 capitals	
	3 [main clauses]	6 commas	
	1 *who/which* clause (w/w)	2 quotation marks	
	4 subject-verb pairs (s v)	1 end mark	
	2 openers	2 usage	Day 4

answering firm bagheera ordered look

at me mowgli. mowgli who wanted to understand

obeyed, and **steadily** looked at he in the eyes

Rewrite It! ____

____

____

____

Learn It!

Transitional Prepositional Phrases

Week 2 you learned that short prepositional openers do not take commas. You also learned that you should not place commas in front of a prepositional phrase. Transitions, however, do take commas. Therefore, when a prepositional phrase functions as a transition, use commas regardless of where it appears in a sentence.

 Place commas around a transitional prepositional phrase.

Some prepositional phrases that function as transitions:

in fact	by the way	for example	of course
in addition	by contrast	for instance	on the other hand

Fix It!   Place commas around a transitional prepositional phrase.

② In fact, Bagheera offered a bull as payment.

Bagheera, in fact, offered a bull as payment.

Bagheera offered a bull as payment, in fact.

Prepositional Phrase or Adverb Clause

These words usually begin prepositional phrases.

aboard	around	between	in	opposite	toward
about	**as**	beyond	inside	out	under
above	at	by	instead of	outside	underneath
according to	**because of**	concerning	into	over	unlike
across	**before**	despite	like	past	**until**
after	behind	down	minus	regarding	unto
against	below	during	near	**since**	up, upon
along	beneath	except	of	through	with
amid	beside	for	off	throughout	within
among	besides	from	on, onto	to	without

Pattern:
preposition + noun
(no verb)

These words usually begin adverb clauses.

when	while	where	**as**	**since**	if	although	**because**
after	**before**	**until**	unless	whenever	whereas	than	

Pattern:
www word +
subject + verb

The words *after, as, because, before, since,* and *until* appear on both lists. When you mark the sentences, consider the patterns.

Prepositional Phrase: <u>As a man's cub</u> Mowgli could remove thorns from paws.

> *As a man's cub* is a prepositional phrase.
> **PATTERN preposition (As) + noun (cub) (no verb)**

Adverb Clause: (As he removed the thorn), Mowgli gained the wolf's trust.

> *As he removed the thorn* is an adverb clause.
> **PATTERN www word (As) + subject (he) + verb (removed)**

Prepositional Phrase or Adverb Clause

Write the prepositional phrase pattern.

____

Write the adverb clause pattern.

____

To determine if a group of words forms a prepositional phrase or an adverb clause, look for a verb. If there is a verb, the words form an adverb clause. If there is not a verb, the words form a prepositional phrase.

Trick: Drop the first word of the phrase or clause in question and look at what is left. If it is a sentence, the group of words forms an adverb clause. If it is not a sentence, the group of words forms a prepositional phrase.

~~after~~ supper

> This does not have a verb. This is a phrase.

~~after~~ they ate supper

> This has a verb (ate). This is a clause.

Decide if the following is a clause or a phrase.

before the summer moon	**phrase**	**clause**
with noble intentions	**phrase**	**clause**
since he could succeed	**phrase**	**clause**
after Mowgli practiced	**phrase**	**clause**
because of his desire	**phrase**	**clause**
when the sun rose	**phrase**	**clause**

Read It! | **Mark It!** | **Fix It!**

1 vocabulary

1 <u>prepositional phrase</u>
2 [main clauses]
1 adverb clause (AC)
3 subject-verb pairs (s v)
1 opener

1 indent
3 capitals
3 commas
2 quotation marks
2 end marks
1 apostrophe
2 usage

looking down after a minute the panther turned

away, although i love you even me cant hold

your **intensely** gaze

Rewrite It! _______________________________________

____

____

____

Read It!	**Mark It!**	**Fix It!**
1 vocabulary	1 <u>prepositional phrase</u>	1 indent
	1 coordinating conjunction (cc)	4 capitals
	3 [main clauses]	4 commas
	2 *that* clauses (that)	3 end marks
	1 adverb clause (AC)	1 apostrophe
	6 subject-verb pairs (s v)	2 usage
	3 openers	

in fact it was true others avoided mowgli,

because they could not stare back, they knew

that he is smart, and could **accomplish** things

that it couldnt

Rewrite It! ____

____

____

____

Read It!	**Mark It!**	**Fix It!**
1 vocabulary	1 coordinating conjunction (cc)	2 capitals
	1 [main clause]	4 commas
	1 *who/which* clause (w/w)	1 end mark
	1 *that* clause (that)	2 apostrophes
	3 subject-verb pairs (s v)	1 usage
	1 opener	

painfully, mowgli **responded** that he didnt know

them thing's which made him angry sad and

disappointed

Rewrite It! ____

____

____

____

Read It!	**Mark It!**	**Fix It!**	Day 4

Read It!	**Mark It!**	**Fix It!**
1 vocabulary	1 <u>prepositional phrase</u>	1 indent
	3 [main clauses]	4 capitals
	2 *that* clauses (that)	5 commas
	1 adverb clause (AC)	4 quotation marks
	6 subject-verb pairs (s v)	2 end marks
		1 apostrophe
		2 usage

by the way that you behaves bagheera warned

they **recognize**, that youre a man, when akela had

an unsuccessful hunt the pack will attack you

Rewrite It! ____

____

____

____

Review It!

Sentence Opener

A **sentence opener** is a descriptive word, phrase, or clause that is added to the beginning of a sentence.

(1) subject

Mowgli rested after a long swim.

begins with the subject of the sentence (may include article or adjective)

(2) prepositional

After a long swim in the jungle pool, Mowgli rested.

begins with a prepositional phrase

PATTERN preposition + noun (no verb)

, if 5 + words or transition

(3) -ly adverb

Certainly, Mowgli rested after his long swim.

begins with an -ly adverb

, if adverb modifies sentence (It was ____ that ____.)

(4) -ing

Swimming for many hours, Mowgli was tired and rested.

begins with a participial phrase

PATTERN -ing word/phrase, main clause

, after phrase

(5) clausal

After he swam in the jungle pool, Mowgli rested.

begins with a www word (subordinating conjunction)

PATTERN www word + subject + verb

, after clause (AC, MC)

(6) vss

The swim exhausted Mowgli.

2–5 words

Sometimes it appears that more than one sentence opener begins a sentence. When this happens, place the comma after the last opener. Number the sentence opener based on the first word of the sentence. For example, the clause *After he swam* and the prepositional phrase *in the jungle pool* come before the main clause *Mowgli rested*. Place the comma after the word *pool*. Label the sentence a #5 clausal opener because the sentence begins with a clause.

Sentence Opener

In this book you have learned six types of sentence openers—six ways to open or begin a sentence. Using different sentence openers makes writing more interesting.

A #1 subject opener is written below. Use the idea of that sentence to write sentences that begin with each type of opener. Add commas where required. There are multiple right answers.

#1 Subject

Mowgli upset the animals when he stared at them during their play.

#2 Prepositional

#3 -ly Adverb

#4 -ing

#5 Clausal

#6 Vss

| **Read It!** | **Mark It!** | **Fix It!** | |

Read It!	**Mark It!**	**Fix It!**
1 vocabulary	3 <u>prepositional phrases</u>	1 indent
	4 [main clauses]	5 capitals
	1 *who/which* clause (w/w)	4 commas
	1 *that* clause (that)	2 quotation marks
	6 subject-verb pairs (s v)	2 end marks
	2 openers	2 apostrophes
		1 usage

suddenly bagheera added i have an idea, that

might work. from the mens huts in the village

take some of their red flower which glow

brightly he knew it's **potential**

Rewrite It! ____

____

____

____

Read It!	**Mark It!**	**Fix It!**
1 vocabulary	2 <u>prepositional phrases</u>	2 capitals
	2 [main clauses]	2 commas
	1 adverb clause (AC)	1 end mark
	3 subject-verb pairs (s v)	1 apostrophe
	2 openers	1 number
		2 usage

because the animal's **dread** fire they had

over 100 different names, for them. red flower

was one

Rewrite It! ______________________________________

____

____

____

____

Read It!	**Mark It!**	**Fix It!**
1 vocabulary	2 coordinating conjunctions (cc)	1 indent
	2 <u>prepositional phrases</u>	4 capitals
	3 [main clauses]	4 commas
	3 subject-verb pairs (s v)	2 end marks
	2 openers	1 apostrophe
		1 usage

obeying bagheera mowgli left, and raced through

the jungle during his run, he heard the packs cry

and he grew **anxiously**

Rewrite It! ____

____

____

____

Read It!	**Mark It!**	**Fix It!**	Day 4
1 vocabulary	1 <u>prepositional phrase</u>	1 indent	
	3 [main clauses]	4 capitals	
	1 adverb clause (AC)	3 commas	
	4 subject-verb pairs (s v)	2 quotation marks	
	1 opener	2 end marks	
		3 usage	

him heard laughter, from the young wolves, as

it **taunted** their aging leader. attack the elk

akela show yours strength

Rewrite It! ____

____

____

____

Learn It!

#4 -ing Opener and -ing Phrase

Week 13 you learned that a **#4 -ing opener** is a sentence that begins with a participial phrase. However, a participial phrase (-ing phrase) does not have to begin a sentence. An -ing phrase can be placed anywhere in a sentence.

Wanting to understand, Mowgli searched Bagheera's eyes.

When an -ing opener begins a sentence,

a comma separates the -ing opener from the main clause, and

the thing after the comma must be the thing doing the inging.

Mowgli searched Bagheera's eyes, wanting to understand.

When an -ing opener does not begin a sentence,

a comma separates the main clause from the -ing phrase.

This book contains only nonessential -ing phrases, which require commas.

Comma

Place commas around a mid-sentence nonessential -ing phrase.
PATTERNS   **-ing word/phrase, main clause**
                    main clause, -ing word/phrase

Fix It!   Read each passage and identify -ing phrases.
                    Add commas around -ing phrases.

The wolves mocked Akela, taunting their aging leader.

Do not include the -ing phrase in the main clause square brackets.

[Akela walked away], ignoring the young wolves.

Phrase

A **phrase** is a group of related words that contains either a noun or a verb, never both.

④-ing

Hearing the pack's cry, [Mowgli was running in the jungle].

[Mowgli had grown anxious], listening to the wolf's cries.

In this book you have learned three types of phrases.

Prepositional Phrase

in the jungle   to the wolf's cries

preposition + noun (no verb)

A prepositional phrase begins with a preposition and ends with a noun.

It adds imagery or information to a sentence because the entire phrase functions as an adjective describing a noun or as an adverb modifying a verb or adjective.

Underline.

after a long prepositional phrase opener (5 + words)
around a transition

Verb Phrase

was running   had grown

helping verb(s) + main verb

A verb phrase includes a main verb (action or linking) and its helping verbs.

It tells what a subject does in a sentence. The helping verbs often indicate the tense.

Mark with a *v*.

Participial (-ing) Phrase

hearing the pack's cry   listening to the wolf's cries

-ing word/phrase, main clause

main clause, -ing word/phrase

A participial phrase begins with a verb form that ends in -ing and usually includes additional words like adverbs, nouns, infinitives, prepositional phrases, or dependent clauses.

It describes a noun because the entire phrase functions as an adjective. This is why the thing (the subject noun) after the comma must be the thing doing the inging.

Mark with a ④ if it begins the sentence. The -ing phrase is outside the *[MC]*.

use commas unless essential

Read It!	**Mark It!**	**Fix It!**	

Read It!	**Mark It!**	**Fix It!**
1 vocabulary	1 coordinating conjunction (cc)	1 indent
	2 <u>prepositional phrases</u>	3 capitals
	2 [main clauses]	3 commas
	1 adverb clause (AC)	1 end mark
	3 subject-verb pairs (s v)	1 apostrophe
	2 openers	1 usage

mowgli heard the snap, of akelas teeth and then

his cry, as the elk kicks him. akela howled in anger

missing his **kill**

Rewrite It! ____

____

____

____

____

Read It!   **Mark It!**   **Fix It!**

1 vocabulary

3 <u>prepositional phrases</u>
2 [main clauses]
1 *who/which* clause (w/w)
1 adverb clause (AC)
4 subject-verb pairs (s v)
2 openers

3 capitals
8 commas
2 end marks
2 usage

fearfully, mowgli dashed **descending** from the

hills, into the farmland, near the village, as he ran

the shrill sounds which terrify him grow fainter

Rewrite It! _______________________________________

____

____

____

Read It!   **Mark It!**   **Fix It!**

1 vocabulary   4 <u>prepositional phrases</u>   1 indent
                    2 [main clauses]   4 capitals
                    2 subject-verb pairs (s v)   4 commas
                    2 openers   1 end mark
                                                          2 apostrophes
                                                          1 usage

beneath the window, of a hut mowgli **crouched**

thinking about bagheeras wise words. by tomorrow,

the wolves claws would reach he

Rewrite It! ____

____

____

____

Read It!	**Mark It!**	**Fix It!**
1 vocabulary	1 coordinating conjunction (cc)	2 capitals
	5 <u>prepositional phrases</u>	4 commas
	2 [main clauses]	1 end mark
	2 subject-verb pairs (s v)	1 apostrophe
	2 openers	1 usage

he pressed his face to the window spotting a fire,

in a large hole. during the night, a woman fed it

with **unfamiliar** black lump's, and gently blew on it

Rewrite It! ____

____

____

____

Learn It!

Adjective

You have learned that an **adjective** describes a noun or pronoun.

Often, two or more adjectives come before a noun. The adjectives are **cumulative** if the first adjective describes the second adjective and the noun that follows. Cumulative adjectives follow this specific order: quantity, opinion, size, age, shape, color, origin, material, purpose.

Comma

Because cumulative adjectives must be arranged in a specific order, the adjectives are not separated with a comma.

 Do not use a comma to separate cumulative adjectives.

Two tests help determine whether the adjectives before a noun are cumulative.

Can you reverse their order?

Can you add *and* between them?

If you answer no, the adjectives are cumulative. Do not use a comma.

adj   *adj*   *n*

They sought shade from the blazing summer sun.

The two adjectives *blazing* and *summer* describe the noun *sun*.

Are they cumulative adjectives? Do they need a comma?

Reverse the order.

... the summer blazing sun. No, you cannot reverse the order.

Add *and* between the adjectives.

... blazing and summer sun. No, you cannot add *and*.

adj   *adj*   *n*

They sought shade from the blazing summer sun.

Blazing and *summer* are cumulative adjectives and are not separated with a comma.

Fix It! Remove the comma between cumulative adjectives.

adj   *adj*

The brilliant, full moon lit the jungle.

Adjectives can be grouped into categories. Cumulative adjectives follow this specific order: quantity, opinion, size, age, shape, color, origin, material, purpose.

Categories	Some Examples		
quantity	three	several	few
opinion	funny	smart	ugly
size	long	huge	tall
age	old	young	ancient
shape	wide	angular	square
color	red	blue	green
origin	Indian	Russian	Catholic
material	wooden	plastic	cotton
purpose	frying (pan)	canoe (paddle)	shade (tree)

Cumulative adjectives build on each other. Mowgli was a *smart Indian* boy. He often played with *three funny young* wolves. If someone said he played with *young funny three* wolves, your ear would tell you that was wrong. That is why the tests work. We have been trained to hear and say adjectives in a certain order, and if you try to rearrange the order of the adjectives, it sounds awkward.

Mowgli was a smart Indian boy.

Smart comes before *Indian* because *opinion* comes before *origin*.

He played with three funny young wolves.

Quantity comes before *opinion*, and *opinion* comes before *age*.

The animals rested under the huge shade tree.

Size comes before *purpose*.

They found a wide wooden canoe paddle.

Shape comes before *material*, and *material* comes before *purpose*.

Read It!	**Mark It!**	**Fix It!**	

Read It!	Mark It!	Fix It!
1 vocabulary	1 <u>prepositional phrase</u>	1 indent
	1 coordinating conjunction (cc)	3 capitals
	2 [main clauses]	4 commas
	1 *that* clause (that)	2 end marks
	1 adverb clause (AC)	1 number
	4 subject-verb pairs (s v)	3 usage
	2 openers	

as the cool morning **mist** appeared mowgli saw

that a child entered the hut the young boy grabs

a pot places 6, black lumps in it and leaves to milk

the cows

Rewrite It! ____

____

____

____

Read It!	**Mark It!**	**Fix It!**	Day 2
1 vocabulary	1 [main clause]	1 capital	
	1 *who/which* clause (w/w)	5 commas	
	1 *that* clause (that)	1 end mark	
	1 adverb clause (AC)	1 usage	
	4 subject-verb pairs (s v)		
	1 opener		

mowgli **concluded**, that he obviously had nothing

to fear, if a helpless, human child who were just a

cub could carry it

Rewrite It! ____

____

____

____

Read It!	**Mark It!**	**Fix It!**
1 vocabulary	1 coordinating conjunction (cc)	1 indent
	4 <u>prepositional phrases</u>	2 capitals
	2 [main clauses]	5 commas
	2 subject-verb pairs (s v)	2 end marks
	2 openers	1 apostrophe
		1 usage

sneaking around the huts corner he grabbed the

pot, from the hand of the **astounded**, small boy, and

left immediate, he now had the source of the

red flower

Rewrite It! ____

____

____

____

Read It!	**Mark It!**	**Fix It!**	Day 4
1 vocabulary	1 <u>prepositional phrase</u>	2 capitals	
	1 [main clause]	2 commas	
	1 *that* clause (that)	1 end mark	
	1 adverb clause (AC)	1 apostrophe	
	3 subject-verb pairs (s v)	1 usage	
	1 opener		

carefully mowgli blew into the pot, as the woman

has done understanding that hed have to feed the

mysterious round lumps **constantly**

Rewrite It! ____

____

____

____

Learn It!

Adjective

You have learned that an **adjective** describes a noun or pronoun.

Often, two or more adjectives come before a noun. Week 17 you learned that adjectives are **cumulative** if the first adjective describes the second adjective and the noun that follows.

The adjectives are **coordinate** if each adjective independently describes the noun that follows.

Comma

Because the order of coordinate adjectives is not important, the adjectives are separated with a comma.

 Use a comma to separate coordinate adjectives.

Two tests help determine whether the adjectives before a noun are coordinate or cumulative.

> Can you reverse their order?

> Can you add *and* between them?

If you answer no, the adjectives are cumulative. Do not use a comma.

If you answer yes, the adjectives are coordinate. Use a comma.

adj   adj   n

Mowgli swam in the cool, cleansing stream.

> The two adjectives *cool* and *cleansing* describe the noun *stream*.

> Are they coordinate adjectives? Do they need a comma?

>> Reverse the order.

>>> ... the cleansing cool stream. Yes, you can reverse the order.

>> Add *and* between the adjectives.

>>> ... the cool and cleansing stream. Yes, you can add *and*.

adj   adj   n

Mowgli swam in the cool, cleansing stream.

> *Cool* and *cleansing* are coordinate adjectives and separated with a comma.

Fix It! Add a comma between coordinate adjectives.

adj   adj

Mowgli pulled a thorn from the tender, inflamed paw.

Last week you learned that adjectives can be grouped into categories.

Categories	Some Examples		
quantity	three	several	few
opinion	funny	smart	ugly
size	long	huge	tall
age	old	young	ancient
shape	wide	angular	square
color	red	blue	green
origin	Indian	Russian	Catholic
material	wooden	plastic	cotton
purpose	frying (pan)	canoe (paddle)	shade (tree)

Coordinate adjectives work equally. They are adjectives that belong in the same category. That is why coordinate adjectives are separated with a comma. It is also why the tests work.

Mowgli was a smart, funny boy.

Both *smart* and *funny* are adjectives of opinion. You can reverse the order or place *and* between them. They are separated with a comma.

The animals rested under the huge, tall tree.

Both *huge* and *tall* are adjectives of size. You can reverse the order or place *and* between them. They are separated with a comma.

Read It!	**Mark It!**	**Fix It!**
1 vocabulary	2 <u>prepositional phrases</u>	1 indent
	2 [main clauses]	4 capitals
	1 *who/which* clause (w/w)	4 commas
	3 subject-verb pairs (s v)	2 end marks
	2 openers	1 usage

scrambling up the jagged rocky hill mowgli

spotted bagheera who eagerly **hailed** them,

mowgli ran toward him

Rewrite It!

Read It!	**Mark It!**	**Fix It!**	
1 vocabulary	2 coordinating conjunctions (cc)	7 capitals	Day 2
	3 <u>prepositional phrases</u>	4 commas	
	2 [main clauses]	1 end mark	
	2 *that* clauses (that)	2 usage	
	4 subject-verb pairs (s v)		
	2 openers		

bagheera informed mowgli, that akela has missed

his kill, and that mowgli were now in danger. during

the night the **senseless** cruel wolves would kill akela,

and hunt for mowgli

Rewrite It! ____

____

____

____

Read It!	**Mark It!**	**Fix It!**
		Day 3

1 vocabulary

1 <u>prepositional phrase</u>
1 [main clause]
1 *that* clause (that)
2 subject-verb pairs (s v)
1 opener

1 indent
1 capital
3 commas
1 end mark
1 apostrophe
2 usage

mowgli showed the dingy dirty pot with their

glowing red coal's exclaiming, that it would

inevitably protect him

Rewrite It! ____

____

____

____

Read It!	**Mark It!**	**Fix It!**	Day 4

Read It!	**Mark It!**	**Fix It!**
1 vocabulary	1 <u>prepositional phrase</u>	3 capitals
	2 [main clauses]	4 commas
	1 *that* clause (that)	2 end marks
	1 adverb clause (AC)	1 apostrophe
	4 subject-verb pairs (s v)	2 usage
	2 openers	

bagheera praised mowgli, he explained that dry

brittle branches' **blossomed** dangerous, when

men place them, into the burning red flower

Rewrite It! ____

____

____

____

Learn It!

Who/Which Clause

Week 4 you began marking *who/which* clauses. There are two types of *who/which* clauses: nonessential and essential.

Nonessential *Who/Which* Clause

Wolves, which normally shun people, hunt in packs.

> Nonessential *W/W*
>
> adds information to the sentence
>
> use commas

A nonessential *who/which* clause adds information to a sentence, but the clause is not needed for the rest of the sentence to make sense.

Use commas to show that the added information can be removed from the sentence.

The nonessential clause may convey important information, but it still will not change the meaning of the rest of the sentence if it is removed.

Wolves, ~~which normally shun people,~~ hunt in packs.

Without the *which* clause, the reader still knows that wolves hunt in packs.

Essential *Who/Which* Clause

Wolves which hunt humans must be killed.

> Essential *W/W*
>
> defines the noun it follows
>
> do not use commas

An essential *who/which* clause defines the noun it follows (in the example, wolves).

Do not use commas because the essential information about the noun cannot be removed from the sentence.

If the essential information about the noun were removed, the overall meaning of the sentence would change.

Wolves ~~which hunt humans~~ must be killed.

Without the *which* clause the sentence says all wolves must be killed. The reader no longer knows which wolves are meant. Removing the clause changes the meaning of the sentence.

Comma

 Place commas around a *who/which* clause if it is nonessential.

 Do not place commas around a *who/which* clause if it is essential (changes the meaning of the sentence).

> Commas give the reader permission to remove the clause from the sentence.

To determine if a *who/which* clause is essential, remove it from the sentence. Does the meaning of the sentence change?

If you answer no, the *who/which* clause is nonessential. Use commas.

If you answer yes, the *who/which* clause is essential. Do not use commas.

Fix It! Insert or remove commas. Follow the comma rules.

w/w s v

Bagheera, (who loved Mowgli), was prepared to defend him.

w/w s v

The wolves, (who sided with Mowgli), distrusted Shere Khan.

Who/Which Clause—Nonessential or Essential

A **nonessential** *who/which* **clause** adds information to a sentence. If the clause is removed, the reader will still understand the overall meaning of the sentence. Use commas.

An **essential** *who/which* **clause** defines the noun it follows. If the clause is removed, the overall meaning of the sentence changes. Do not use commas.

Read each sentence and decide if the *who/which* clause is nonessential or essential.
   Circle the correct answer.
   Insert commas where needed.

Jungles which are found all over the world are most common near the equator.

nonessential   essential

The jungle is home to many types of plants which include palm trees, vines, moss, and ferns.

nonessential   essential

Plants which give off poisonous toxins cannot be eaten by man or animal.

nonessential   essential

The story of a boy who lived among animals in the jungle first appeared in *The Jungle Book*.

nonessential   essential

Rudyard Kipling who wrote *The Jungle Book* introduced the term "law of the jungle."

nonessential   essential

Wolves which raise human children are merely fictional.

nonessential   essential

Read It!	**Mark It!**	**Fix It!**
1 vocabulary	1 coordinating conjunction (cc)	1 indent
	1 <u>prepositional phrase</u>	3 capitals
	2 [main clauses]	5 commas
	1 *who/which* clause (w/w)	1 end mark
	3 subject-verb pairs (s v)	2 apostrophes
	2 openers	1 usage

at the groups, afternoon meeting, mowgli arrived

feeling **capable**, and unafraid. the animal's, who

wanted to kill him, whispered impatient

Rewrite It! _______________________________

____

____

____

____

Read It!	**Mark It!**	**Fix It!**
1 vocabulary	1 [main clause]	4 capitals
	1 *who/which* clause (w/w)	3 commas
	1 *that* clause (that)	1 end mark
	3 subject-verb pairs (s v)	1 usage
	1 opener	

signaling, that it was time to begin the meeting

akela **ascended** a flat square rock, which were called

council rock

Rewrite It! ____

____

____

____

Read It!	**Mark It!**	**Fix It!**
1 vocabulary	1 coordinating conjunction (cc)	6 capitals
	3 <u>prepositional phrases</u>	3 commas
	2 [main clauses]	2 end marks
	2 *who/which* clauses (w/w)	2 usage
	4 subject-verb pairs (s v)	
	2 openers	

the wolves who followed shere khan circle around

him, and wait for him to speak silently bagheera

lay beside mowgli who **clutched** the clay, fire pot

Rewrite It!

Read It!	**Mark It!**	**Fix It!**	Day 4
1 vocabulary	1 coordinating conjunction (cc)	1 indent	
	2 [main clauses]	5 capitals	
	1 *who/which* clause (w/w)	4 commas	
	1 adverb clause (AC)	1 end mark	
	4 subject-verb pairs (s v)	1 usage	
	1 opener		

when the pack was quiet shere khan starts to

speak but mowgli interrupted him **challenging**

the wolves, who threatened akela

Rewrite It! ____

____

____

____

____

Review It!

Conjunction

A **conjunction** connects words, phrases, or clauses.

In this book you have learned two types of conjunctions.

Coordinating Conjunction (cc)

ACRONYM FANBOYS

connects the same type of words, phrases, or clauses

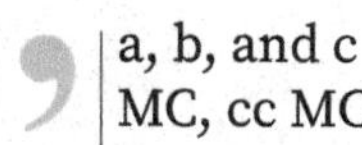 a, b, and c
MC, cc MC

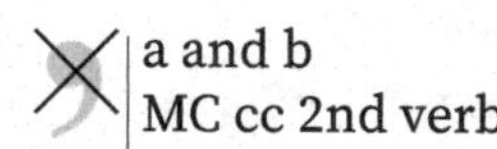 a and b
MC cc 2nd verb

cc
____
for, and, nor, but,
or, yet, so

Subordinating Conjunction (www word)

ACRONYM www.asia.b + others

connects an adverb clause to a main clause

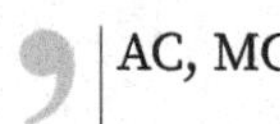 AC, MC

 MC AC

www word
____
when, while,
where, as, since,
if, although,
because, after,
before, until,
unless, whenever,
whereas, than

Fill in the blanks with conjunctions. Add commas where needed.

The cubs chatted _________ grumbled about Mowgli's place in the pack.
          cc

"He will die in the winter rains _________ he stays."
          www

"_________ we are protected by our fur Mowgli has no fur."
  www

"He will freeze in the winter _________ scorch under the summer sun."
          cc

"He is weak _________ we should not fear him."
      cc

"Let him run with us _________ he is harmless."
        www

"Let him run with us _________ he can't harm us."
        cc

"Mowgli will run with us we'll get the bull _________ no one will be hurt.
          cc

Read It!	**Mark It!**	**Fix It!**
1 vocabulary	1 coordinating conjunction (cc)	3 capitals
	2 <u>prepositional phrases</u>	4 commas
	3 [main clauses]	2 quotation marks
	1 *who/which* clause (w/w)	3 end marks
	4 subject-verb pairs (s v)	1 apostrophe
		1 usage

coward's are you ruled by a tiger must you obey

this **clumsy** overgrown cat who is no better than a

bully you could of shown courage, and kindness

Rewrite It! ____

____

____

____

Read It!	**Mark It!**	**Fix It!**	Day 2

Read It!	**Mark It!**	**Fix It!**
1 vocabulary	6 [main clauses]	2 indents
	6 subject-verb pairs (s v)	6 capitals
	3 openers	5 commas
		4 quotation marks
		4 end marks
		2 apostrophes
		2 usage

glaring at himself some yelled keep silent

mans cub others begged let him speak

hes kept our law, the **tension** grows

Rewrite It! ____

____

____

____

Read It!	**Mark It!**	**Fix It!**
1 vocabulary	2 coordinating conjunctions (cc)	1 indent
	3 <u>prepositional phrases</u>	3 capitals
	3 [main clauses]	5 commas
	1 *that* clause (that)	2 end marks
	4 subject-verb pairs (s v)	1 number
	2 openers	2 usage

wearily, akela stated that for 12, successful years

he faithfully led his pack proving his strength,

and skill until last night he has always led them to

the kill and never has anyone been hurt

Rewrite It! ____

____

____

____

| **Read It!** | **Mark It!** | **Fix It!** | |

Read It!

1 vocabulary

Mark It!

1 coordinating conjunction (cc)
2 prepositional phrases
2 [main clauses]
1 *that* clause (that)
1 adverb clause (AC)
4 subject-verb pairs (s v)
1 opener

Fix It!

1 capital
4 commas
1 end mark
1 apostrophe
1 number

since he missed his attack yesterday the jungles,

firm law stated, that they could kill him now but

by the same law they must **approach** 1 at a time

Rewrite It! ____

____

____

____

Learn It!

Who/Which Clause

You have learned that a ***who/which* clause** is a dependent clause that begins with the word *who* or *which* and follows the noun it describes. Use the pronoun *who* when referring to people, personified animals, and pets. Use the pronoun *which* when referring to things, animals, and places.

The pronoun *who* has three forms: *who, whom, whose.*

Use *who* when the subject of a *who* clause is *who.*

w/w s   v

Shere Khan circled the wolves, (who felt threatened).

> A *who* clause is used because *wolves* refer to personified animals.
> The *who* clause describes *wolves,* the noun it follows.
> The wolves felt threatened.
> The subject of the *who* clause is *who.* Begin the clause with *who.*

Use *whom* when the subject of a *who* clause is not *who.*

w/w   s   v

Shere Khan circled the wolves, (whom he threatened).

> A *who* clause is used because *wolves* refers to personified animals.
> The *who/which* clause describes *wolves,* the noun it follows.
> He threatened the wolves.
> The subject of the *who* clause is *he.* Begin the clause with *whom.*

Use *whose* when the first word of either a *who* or a *which* clause functions as an adjective.

w/w   s v

Shere Khan circled the wolves, (whose loyalty he desired).

> The *who/which* clause describes *wolves,* the noun it follows.
> He desired the wolves' loyalty. Whose loyalty? *whose* (wolves')
> The first word of the clause functions as an adjective. Begin the clause with *whose.*

This week focus on *who* and *whom.*

Next week focus on *whose.*

Mark It! Place parentheses around the *who/which* clause and write *w/w* above the word *who* or *which.* Write *v* above each verb and *s* above each subject.

Fix It! Place a line through the incorrect pronoun and write the correct word above it.
Use *who* when the subject of the *who* clause is *who.*
Use *whom* when the subject of the *who* clause is not *who.*

w/w s   v
who

Mowgli listened to Akela, (~~whom~~ spoke truth).

w/w   s   v
whom

Mowgli listened to Akela, (~~who~~ he respected).

#4 -ing Opener

A **#4 -ing opener** is a sentence that begins with a participial phrase.

Week 13 you learned the pattern and the rule for the #4 -ing opener.

> **PATTERN** -ing word/phrase, main clause

The thing after the comma must be the thing doing the inging.

Wanting to understand, Mowgli searched Bagheera's eyes.

> *Mowgli* is the thing (subject of main clause) after the comma. *Mowgli* is doing the *wanting*.

Illegal #4 Opener

An illegal #4 is grammatically incorrect. It occurs when the thing after the comma (subject of main clause) is not the thing doing the inging. A sentence with an illegal #4 opener does not make sense.

Leading the wolves for years, the pack was served faithfully.

> The pack is not doing the leading; Akela is. The sentence does not make sense. The sentence must be rewritten so *Akela* is the thing after the comma.

Leading the wolves for years, Akela served the pack faithfully.

> *Akela* is the thing (subject of main clause) after the comma. *Akela* is doing the *leading*. This is a grammatically correct, legal #4 opener.

Find It!   Check that the thing (subject of main clause) after the comma is the thing doing the inging.

Fix It!   Rewrite if necessary.

Roaring at the wolf cubs, ~~they were urged by~~ *urged them* Shere Khan to fight Akela.

There is often more than one way to rewrite an illegal #4 sentence.

Read It!	**Mark It!**	**Fix It!**
1 vocabulary	2 <u>prepositional phrases</u>	2 indents
	2 [main clauses]	2 capitals
	1 adverb clause (AC)	3 commas
	3 subject-verb pairs (s v)	1 end mark
	2 openers	1 illegal #4 opener

at that moment, no one spoke, because no **solitary**

wolf wanted to fight Akela to the death. breaking the

silence the wolves heard Shere Khan roar

Rewrite It! ____

____

____

____

____

Read It!	**Mark It!**	**Fix It!**	Day 2
1 vocabulary	3 <u>prepositional phrases</u>	5 capitals	
	3 [main clauses]	2 commas	
	1 *who/which* clause (w/w)	2 quotation marks	
	1 adverb clause (AC)	2 end marks	
	5 subject-verb pairs (s v)	1 apostrophe	
		1 usage	

who cares about the old wolf it's the mans cub

who i despise. unless you give him to me now

i will never again share fresh **succulent** bones

with you

Rewrite It! ____

____

____

____

Read It!	**Mark It!**	**Fix It!**
1 vocabulary	1 coordinating conjunction (cc)	1 indent
	2 prepositional phrases	3 capitals
	3 [main clauses]	6 commas
	1 *that* clause (that)	2 end marks
	4 subject-verb pairs (s v)	1 apostrophe
	3 openers	1 illegal #4 opener

rising to his feet an announcement was made by

Akela. he stated, that Mowgli had shared their food,

and had tended their sick, **recently** hed driven

game, for them

Rewrite It! _______________________________________

____

____

____

Read It!	**Mark It!**	**Fix It!**	
			Day 4

Read It!	**Mark It!**	**Fix It!**
1 vocabulary	1 coordinating conjunction	1 indent
	2 <u>prepositional phrases</u>	1 capital
	1 [main clause]	2 commas
	1 *that* clause (that)	1 end mark
	1 *who/which* clause (w/w)	1 apostrophe
	3 subject-verb pairs (s v)	2 usage
	1 opener	

growling **menacingly** Bagheera threatened that

the loyal wolves and him would fight for Mowgli

who he had purchased with a bull many year's ago

Rewrite It! ____

____

____

____

Learn It!

Who/Which Clause

A **who/which clause** is a dependent clause that begins with the word *who* or *which*. Last week you learned that the pronoun *who* has three forms: *who, whom, whose.*

Use *who* when the subject of a *who* clause is *who*.

Use *whom* when the subject of a *who* clause is not *who*.

Use *whose* when the first word of either a *who* or a *which* clause functions as an adjective.

> The pronoun *whose* is a possessive pronoun that functions as an adjective. Like *who* and *whom*, the pronoun *whose* can begin a clause that refers to people, personified animals, and pets. Like *which* the pronoun *whose* can begin a clause that refers to things, animals, and places.

Shere Khan circled the wolves, (whose loyalty he desired).

> The *who/which* clause describes *wolves*, the noun it follows.
> He desired the wolves' loyalty. Whose loyalty? *whose* (wolves')
> The first word of the clause functions as an adjective. Begin the clause with *whose*.

The jungle, (whose foliage is dense), has lots of rainfall.

> The *who/which* clause describes *jungle*, the noun it follows.
> The jungle's foliage is dense. Whose foliage? *whose* (jungle's)
> The first word of the clause functions as an adjective. Begin the clause with *whose*.

Homophone

A **homophone** is a word that sounds like another word but is spelled differently and has a different meaning. Do not confuse *whose* with *who's*.

Whose is a possessive pronoun that functions as an adjective.

Who's is a contraction for *who is*. It includes both a subject (who) and a verb (is). You can use *who's* to begin a *who* clause only when the subject of the clause is *who*.

Mark It! Place parentheses around the *who/which* clause and write **w/w** above the word *who* or *which*. Write **v** above each verb and **s** above each subject.

Fix It! Place a line through the incorrect pronoun and write the correct word above it. Use *whose* when the first word of a *who/which* clause functions as an adjective. Use *who's* for the contraction *who is*.

Mowgli listened to Akela, (~~who~~ support comforted him).

The wolf (~~whose~~ able to attack Akela) will lead the pack.

Week 4 you learned that pronouns have 3 cases: subjective, objective, and possessive. Here is a portion of the chart on page 20.

3 cases	*Subjective* function as	*Objective* function as	*Possessive* function as
	subject subject complement	object of preposition direct object indirect object	adjective
	he	him	his
	who	whom	whose

The pronoun *he* has three forms: *he, him, his.* Use *he* when the pronoun functions as a subject, *him* when the pronoun functions as an object, and *his* when the pronoun functions as an adjective in order to show ownership.

The pronoun *who* also has three forms: *who, whom, whose.* Use *who* when the pronoun functions as a subject, *whom* when the pronoun functions as an object, and *whose* when the pronoun functions as an adjective in order to show ownership.

Read It!	**Mark It!**	**Fix It!**
1 vocabulary	1 <u>prepositional phrase</u>	1 indent
	1 [main clause]	1 capital
	1 *who/which* clause (w/w)	4 commas
	2 subject-verb pairs (s v)	1 end mark
	1 opener	1 illegal #4 opener

grumbling loudly the bull whose dry brittle bones

had been lying around, for a **decade** did not matter

to the pack

Rewrite It! ____

____

____

____

Read It!	**Mark It!**	**Fix It!**	Day 2
1 vocabulary	1 coordinating conjunction (cc)	2 capitals	
	3 <u>prepositional phrases</u>	5 commas	
	3 [main clauses]	2 end marks	
	1 *who/which* clause (w/w)	3 usage	
	2 adverb clauses (AC)		
	6 subject-verb pairs (s v)		
	1 opener		

because Bagheera sought justice he asked the wolves

who's **vows** had been important if they still cared,

about their vows do they choose for them

or did they obey this killer of cattle

Rewrite It! ____

____

____

____

Read It!	**Mark It!**	**Fix It!**
1 vocabulary	2 prepositional phrases	1 indent
	2 [main clauses]	2 capitals
	1 *who/which* clause (w/w)	3 commas
	2 *that* clauses (that)	2 end marks
	5 subject-verb pairs (s v)	1 apostrophe
	2 openers	1 usage

the tiger **protested**, that wolves could not run,

with a mans cub he demanded that they give him

Mowgli who he had hated for so long

Rewrite It! _______________________________________

____

____

____

Read It!	**Mark It!**	**Fix It!**
1 vocabulary	5 <u>prepositional phrases</u>	1 indent
	2 [main clauses]	2 capitals
	1 *that* clause (that)	4 commas
	1 adverb clause (AC)	2 end marks
	4 subject-verb pairs (s v)	1 apostrophe
	2 openers	1 usage

with tenderness, Akela replied that in everything,

but blood Mowgli had been their brother hed

maintained the law, of the jungle better than any,

of they had

Rewrite It! ______________________________________

____

____

____

Learn It!

That Clause

A **that clause** is a dependent clause that begins with the word *that*.

Week 7 you learned a *that* clause is a dependent clause because it does not express a complete thought. It cannot stand alone as a sentence. A *that* clause is easy to recognize because it begins with the word *that*.

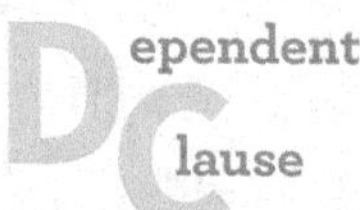

That Clause

Pattern:
that + subject + verb

First Word:
that
(may be invisible)

Commas:
none

Marking:
that

    s   *v*   **that**   *s*   *v*   *v*

[Akela knew] (that they would fight him to the death).

This sentence has two subject-verb pairs: a main clause and a *that* clause.

Invisible *That* Clause

An **invisible *that* clause** occurs when the word *that* is implied, not stated directly. The word *that* is invisible.

    s   *v*   *s*   *v*   *v*

Akela knew they would fight him to the death.

This sentence has two subject-verb pairs and appears to have two main clauses.

    s   *v*   *s*   *v*   *v*

Akela knew. They would fight him to the death.

If you insert a period, the sentences do not make sense. A main clause must express a complete thought. What did Akela know? These words must be in the same sentence in order to make sense.

    s   *v*   **that**   *s*   *v*   *v*

[Akela knew] **(that)** they would fight him to the death).

The word *that* is implied, not stated directly. It is not written in the sentence. The second clause is still considered a dependent *that* clause. You can confirm this by inserting the word *that* into the sentence: Akela knew (that) they would fight him to the death.

Comma

✕ *That* clauses do not take commas.

Mark It!   Place parentheses around the invisible *that* clause and write **that** where the word *that* could be inserted. Write *v* above each verb and *s* above each subject.

    s   *v*   **that**   *s*   *v*

This was the fight **(**Shere Khan wanted to win**)**.

Read It!	**Mark It!**	**Fix It!**
1 vocabulary	2 <u>prepositional phrases</u>	2 capitals
	2 [main clauses]	5 commas
	1 *who/which* clause (w/w)	2 end marks
	1 *that* clause (that)	3 usage
	4 subject-verb pairs (s v)	
	2 openers	

the wolves do not admit, that Shere Khan

influences them, secret they had crept, into

the villages, of men whose cattle they had killed

Rewrite It! _______________________________

____

____

____

____

Read It!	**Mark It!**	**Fix It!**	Day 2
1 vocabulary	1 coordinating conjunction (cc)	1 indent	
	2 <u>prepositional phrases</u>	1 capital	
	2 [main clauses]	6 commas	
	1 *that* clause (that)	1 end mark	
	2 adverb clauses (AC)	1 apostrophe	
	5 subject-verb pairs (s v)	1 usage	
	1 opener		

with sorrow, Akela knew, he had to die

but if they **restored** the mans cub, to their village

he would not fight them, when the time came

Rewrite It! ____

____

____

____

Read It!	**Mark It!**	**Fix It!**
1 vocabulary	1 coordinating conjunction (cc)	2 capitals
	3 <u>prepositional phrases</u>	6 commas
	2 [main clauses]	2 end marks
	1 *who/which* clause (w/w)	1 usage
	1 *that* clause (that)	
	1 adverb clause (AC)	
	5 subject-verb pairs (s v)	
	2 openers	

he requested, they **consider** his plan, if they

agreed they would save some lives, and would not

shame the pack, for the killing of an innocent, human

brother, whose been bought into the pack

Rewrite It! ______________________________

____

____

____

____

Read It!	**Mark It!**	**Fix It!**
1 vocabulary	3 <u>prepositional phrases</u>	1 indent
	1 [main clause]	1 capital
	1 *who/which* clause (w/w)	3 commas
	2 subject-verb pairs (s v)	1 end mark
	1 opener	1 usage

complaining against Mowgli most, of the wolves

gathered around Shere Khan who's tail was beginning

to whip **furiously**

Rewrite It! _______________________________________

____

____

____

Learn It!

Unnecessary Commas with Subject-Verb Pairs

Every clause contains a subject-verb pair.

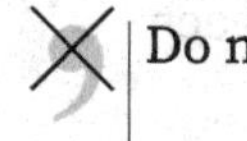 Do not put a comma between a subject and its verb.

S   *V*
Mother Wolf, loved Mowgli.

Remove this comma because you do not put a comma between a subject and its verb.

S   *V*
Some of the wolves still, supported Mowgli.

Remove this comma because you do not put a comma between a subject and its verb even if there are words between the subject and its verb.

S   *V*
Shere Khan, who hated Mowgli, deceived the wolves.

You just learned you should not put a comma between a subject and its verb. However, you have also learned this rule: Place commas around a nonessential *who/which* clause. When two comma rules contradict, follow the rule that says use a comma.

Fix It!   Remove a comma between a subject and its verb.

S   *V*   *V*
Mowgli, could not understand their hatred.

Unnecessary Comma Rules

You have now learned several places where commas are unnecessary.

 The key to punctuating sentences correctly is to think about parts of speech and the structure of your sentences.

Subject-Verb Pair

> Do not put a comma between a subject and its verb.

Coordinating Conjunction

> Do not use a comma before a cc when it connects two items in a series (unless main clauses). **a and b**
> Do not use a comma before a cc when it connects two verbs. **MC CC 2ND VERB**

Prepositional Phrase

> Do not put a comma in front of a prepositional phrase.

Who/Which Clause and Participial (-ing) Phrase

> Do not use commas when the phrase or clause is essential.
> > Essential means it changes the meaning of the sentence.

Adverb Clause

> Do not use a comma before an adverb clause that follows a main clause. **MC AC**

That Clause

> Do not use a comma before a *that* clause.

Adjectives

> Do not use a comma to separate cumulative adjectives.
> > Cumulative means the adjectives must be arranged in a specific order.
> > You cannot reverse their order or add *and* between them.

Interjection

> Do not use a comma after an interjection that expresses strong emotion.
> > Use an exclamation mark instead.

Quotations

> Do not use a comma after a quoted question or quoted exclamation.
> The question mark or exclamation mark replaces the comma.
> > **"Quote?" attribution.**   **"Quote!" attribution.**

Sentence Openers

> (2) **prepositional**   Do not use a comma if fewer than 5 words.
>
> (3) **-ly adverb**   Do not use a comma if an -ly adverb modifies the verb.

There is always a reason a comma is necessary.

Follow the comma rules.

Read It!	**Mark It!**	**Fix It!**
1 vocabulary	2 coordinating conjunctions (cc)	1 indent
	3 <u>prepositional phrases</u>	2 capitals
	2 [main clauses]	4 commas
	2 subject-verb pairs (s v)	2 end marks
	2 openers	2 apostrophes

murmuring to Mowgli Bagheera, encouraged him
to stand for justice, they would fight for Mowglis
and Akelas lives, and teach Shere Khan a lesson

Rewrite It! ____

____

____

____

____

Read It!	**Mark It!**	**Fix It!**
1 vocabulary	1 coordinating conjunction (cc)	1 indent
	2 [main clauses]	2 capitals
	1 adverb clause (AC)	6 commas
	3 subject-verb pairs (s v)	1 end mark
	2 openers	1 illegal #4 opener

inwardly Mowgli, felt rage, and sorrow, because no wolf, had ever shown him such hatred. holding out the warm, fire pot the burning coals empowered Mowgli

Rewrite It! ____

____

____

____

Read It!	**Mark It!**	**Fix It!**
1 vocabulary	1 coordinating conjunction (cc)	2 capitals
	1 <u>prepositional phrase</u>	4 commas
	4 [main clauses]	3 quotation marks
	2 *that* clauses (that)	2 end marks
	6 subject-verb pairs (s v)	1 apostrophe
		2 usage

cease this foolish talk he ordered. to my

lifes end, I, would have stayed a wolf but I know

you speaks the truth declaring that I be a man

No closing quotation mark because quote continues.

Rewrite It! ____

____

____

____

Read It!	**Mark It!**	**Fix It!**	Day 4
1 vocabulary	3 [main clauses]	2 capitals	
	1 *who/which* clause	4 commas	
	1 *that* clause (that)	1 quotation mark	
	1 adverb clause (AC)	3 end marks	
	6 subject-verb pairs (s v)	2 apostrophes	
		2 usage	

No opening quotation mark because quote continues.

because I now **comprehend** Im human

I, no longer calls you brother's look

I hold the mighty, red flower whom you fear

Rewrite It! ____

____

____

____

Review It!

An **adjective** describes a noun or pronoun. Often, two or more adjectives come before a noun. If the adjectives are coordinate, they need a comma. If they are cumulative, they do not need a comma.

Coordinate Adjectives

Each adjective independently describes the noun it follows.

You can reverse their order or add *and* between them.

Cumulative Adjectives

The first adjective describes the second adjective and the noun that follows.

Cumulative adjectives follow this specific order: quantity, opinion, size, age, shape, color, origin, material, purpose.

Test the adjectives to determine if they are coordinate or cumulative.

Circle the correct answer.

Insert commas where needed.

Two tests:

Can you reverse their order?

Can you add *and* between them?

If yes, the adjectives are coordinate. Use a comma.

If no, the adjectives are cumulative. Do not use a comma.

the hungry bald eagle	**coordinate**	**cumulative**
a boastful active tiger	**coordinate**	**cumulative**
a shiny smooth pebble	**coordinate**	**cumulative**
a noisy young monkey	**coordinate**	**cumulative**
a stubborn gray donkey	**coordinate**	**cumulative**
the muddy swift stream	**coordinate**	**cumulative**

Commas

There is always a reason a comma is necessary. Follow the comma rules.

When two comma rules contradict, follow the rule that says to use a comma.

 The key to adding commas is to think about parts of speech and the structure of your sentences.

Coordinating Conjunction

Use a comma before a cc when it connects two main clauses. **MC, cc MC**
Use commas to separate three or more items in a series. **a, b, and c**

Who/Which Clause and Participial (-ing) Phrase

Use commas unless essential.
Essential means it changes the meaning of the sentence.

Adjectives

Use a comma to separate coordinate adjectives.
Coordinate means you can reverse their order or add *and* between them.

Interjection

Use a comma after an interjection that does not express strong emotion.

Noun of Direct Address (NDA)

Use commas.

Quotations

Use a comma to separate an attribution from a direct quote.
"Quote," attribution.
Attribution, "Quote."
"Quote," attribution, "rest of quoted sentence."

Sentence Openers

②　**prepositional**　Use a comma if 5 + words or transition.
preposition + noun (no verb)

③　**-ly adverb**　Use a comma if an -ly adverb modifies the sentence.
It was _____ that _____.

④　**-ing**　Use a comma after the phrase.
-ing word/phrase, main clause

⑤　**clausal**　Use a comma after the clause. **AC, MC**
www word + subject + verb,

 Do not use unnecessary commas.

Read It!	**Mark It!**	**Fix It!**	Day 1
1 vocabulary	3 <u>prepositional phrases</u>	1 indent	
	2 [main clauses]	2 capitals	
	1 *who/which* clause (w/w)	6 commas	
	3 subject-verb pairs (s v)	1 end mark	
	2 openers	2 usage	

at once, he throws the glowing, red coals on the

ground **igniting** some dried moss. fearfully, the

wolves which hair stood on end backed away

Rewrite It! ____

____

____

____

Read It!	**Mark It!**	**Fix It!**	

Read It!	**Mark It!**	**Fix It!**
1 vocabulary	1 coordinating conjunction (cc)	1 capital
	4 <u>prepositional phrases</u>	5 commas
	1 [main clause]	1 end mark
	1 adverb clause (AC)	2 usage
	2 subject-verb pairs (s v)	
	1 opener	

thrusting a dry dead branch into the fire, until they

light Mowgli whirled it above his head looked at

Bagheera and moved toward the **cowering** wolves

Rewrite It! ____

____

____

____

Read It!	**Mark It!**	**Fix It!**
1 vocabulary	1 coordinating conjunction (cc)	1 indent
	2 prepositional phrases	2 capitals
	4 [main clauses]	5 commas
	1 adverb clause (AC)	4 quotation marks
	5 subject-verb pairs (s v)	1 end mark
		2 usage

since you control the pack Mowgli whispered

Bagheera you can save Akela from death. he have

consistently been your friend so now you, can repay

himself for his kindness

Rewrite It! _______________________________________

____

____

____

Read It!	**Mark It!**	**Fix It!**	
			Day 4

Read It!	**Mark It!**	**Fix It!**
1 vocabulary	2 <u>prepositional phrases</u>	1 indent
	4 [main clauses]	3 capitals
	1 *that* clause (that)	2 commas
	5 subject-verb pairs (s v)	3 end marks
	4 openers	1 apostrophe
		1 illegal #4

standing alone the burning branch was held high

in the air by Mowgli the shadow's **quivered**. Akela

hoped, Mowgli would be merciful he looked

straight at him

Rewrite It! ____

____

____

____

Learn It!

Commas

Starting this week, the passages do not contain any commas. Follow the comma rules learned throughout the year to insert commas where they belong.

Compound Adjective

A **compound adjective** is a single adjective made up of two or more words.

Use a hyphen when two or more words come before a noun they describe and act as a single idea.

Bagheera was a quick-witted panther.

The words *quick* and *witted* are not separate adjectives describing the noun. Bagheera was not a quick panther and a witted panther. Together the words act as a single idea and form a compound adjective. Use a hyphen.

Fix It!   Add a hyphen to form a compound adjective in front of a noun.

Mowgli swam in the sun-filled pools.

Read It!	**Mark It!**	**Fix It!**
1 vocabulary	1 coordinating conjunction (cc)	1 indent
	2 <u>prepositional phrases</u>	1 capital
	2 [main clauses]	2 commas
	1 *that* clause (that)	1 end mark
	1 adverb clause (AC)	1 hyphen
	4 subject-verb pairs (s v)	1 usage
	1 opener	

because Mowgli was no longer welcome

in the jungle he had to leave but he **pledged**

that he would be more compassionate than them

cold blooded wolves

Rewrite It! _______________________________________

____

____

____

____

Read It!	**Mark It!**	**Fix It!**
1 vocabulary	1 <u>prepositional phrase</u>	2 commas
	1 [main clause]	1 end mark
	1 *who/which* clause (w/w)	1 apostrophe
	1 adverb clause (AC)	1 hyphen
	3 subject-verb pairs (s v)	1 usage
	1 opener	

Mowgli who were a self confident brother wouldnt

betray them to men as they had cruelly betrayed him

Rewrite It! ____

____

____

____

____

Read It! | **Mark It!** | **Fix It!**

Read It!	Mark It!	Fix It!
1 vocabulary	1 coordinating conjunction (cc)	1 indent
	4 <u>prepositional phrases</u>	2 capitals
	2 [main clauses]	3 commas
	1 *who/which* clause (w/w)	2 end marks
	1 *that* clause (that)	1 hyphen
	4 subject-verb pairs (s v)	1 number
	2 openers	2 usage

in addition Mowgli knew he still had 1 **debt**

to pay boldly he approached Shere Khan whom was

staring nervous at the flames and grabbed the

strong willed tiger by the hair on his chin

Rewrite It! ______________________________

____

____

____

____

Read It!	**Mark It!**	**Fix It!**	Day 4
1 vocabulary	3 <u>prepositional phrases</u>	1 capital	
	1 [main clause]	2 commas	
	1 subject-verb pair (s v)	1 end mark	
	1 opener	1 apostrophe	
		1 hyphen	
		1 usage	

with his ear's against his head Shere Khan **frantically**

shut their eyes whimpering because of the blazing hot

branch

Rewrite It! ____

____

____

____

Review It!

Commas

Starting this week, the Fix It! section no longer indicates how many commas are needed in each passage. Insert commas where needed, keeping in mind that some passages will not require any commas. You must determine where to put commas based on comma rules. This is what you must do with your own writing too since no one tells you how many commas you need in the sentences that you write.

Using the list below, tell which comma rule is applied in each sentence.

A	MC, cc MC	**H**	#2 opener 5 + words
B	a, b, and c	**I**	#2 opener transitional
C	nonessential *who/which*	**J**	#3 opener sentence adverb (It was ____ that ____)
D	coordinate adjectives		
E	mild interjection	**K**	#4 opener -ing
F	NDA	**L**	#5 opener clausal
G	"Quote," attribution, "quote"		

F "Mowgli, try this raw meat."

____ "Oh, I prefer to eat it cooked."

____ "Cooked meat takes time," the cubs replied, "and tastes awful!"

____ Mowgli liked dandelion greens, nuts, and seeds.

____ When he could climb trees, he learned to collect honey.

____ Clearly, he gained many skills in the jungle.

____ He could hear the scratch of a bat's claws, and he could interpret an owl's hoot.

____ At sunrise early one morning, he ran to the lake.

____ He watched a patient, clever bear snag salmon in its claws.

____ Casting out a baited line, Mowgli also caught fish.

____ His favorite was salmon, which swarmed in groups.

____ Of course, he knew what it meant when they swam upstream.

Read It! | **Mark It!** | **Fix It!**

1 vocabulary

1 <u>prepositional phrase</u>
1 [main clause]
1 *that* clause (that)
2 adverb clauses (AC)
4 subject-verb pairs (s v)

1 indent
1 capital
? commas
1 quotation mark
1 end mark
1 usage

this coward **confidently** bragged he would

destroy myself at the next meeting because he had

not killed me when I was a cub

No closing quotation mark because quote continues.

Rewrite It! ____

____

____

____

____

Read It!	**Mark It!**	**Fix It!**	Day 2
1 vocabulary	1 coordinating conjunction (cc)	3 capitals	
	1 <u>prepositional phrase</u>	? commas	
	2 [main clauses]	1 quotation mark	
	1 adverb clause (AC)	2 end marks	
	3 subject-verb pairs (s v)	1 hyphen	
		2 usage	

No opening quotation mark because quote continues.

as a man i will not **tolerate** rude nasty cowards

and self serving bullies if you moves a whisker

you will feel them flames

Rewrite It! ______________________________________

____

____

____

Read It!	**Mark It!**	**Fix It!**
1 vocabulary	2 coordinating conjunctions (cc)	1 indent
	5 [main clauses]	4 capitals
	5 subject-verb pairs (s v)	? commas
	1 opener	4 quotation marks
		4 end marks
		1 apostrophe
		1 illegal #4

holding Shere Khan's chin the tiger trembled and

whined leave now Mowgli **commanded**

never come back or ill stop you forever

Rewrite It! ____

____

____

____

Read It!	Mark It!	Fix It!	
			Day 4
1 vocabulary	1 coordinating conjunction (cc)	2 indents	
	4 <u>prepositional phrases</u>	2 capitals	
	3 [main clauses]	? commas	
	1 *who/which* clause (w/w)	3 end marks	
	4 subject-verb pairs (s v)	2 usage	
	3 openers		

growling in terror Shere Khan fled into the jungle

Mowgli looked at Akela who he **respected** he

then turns positioning himself between Akela and

the other wolves

Rewrite It! ______________________________

____

____

____

____

Learn It!

Unclear Pronoun

Week 2 you learned that a pronoun replaces a noun in order to avoid repetition. An antecedent is the word the pronoun refers to.

The pronoun should clearly refer back to its antecedent. If the pronoun is unclear, use the person's name.

Baloo asked Mowgli if he wanted to swim.

> *He* follows the noun *Mowgli.* It is clear that *he* refers to Mowgli. This is a clear pronoun.

Baloo taught Mowgli how to climb trees and gather honey.

He loved to eat it raw.

> Even though *he* follows the noun *Mowgli,* it is unclear whether *he* refers to Baloo or Mowgli. This is an unclear pronoun.

Baloo taught Mowgli how to climb trees and gather honey.

Mowgli loved to eat it raw.

> Now it is clear who loved to eat raw honey.

Fix It!   Place a line through the unclear pronoun and write the person's name above it.

Mowgli

Afraid of Mowgli, Shere Khan fled into the jungle. ~~He~~

saved Akela.

Read It!	**Mark It!**	**Fix It!**
1 vocabulary	1 <u>prepositional phrase</u>	1 capital
	1 [main clause]	? commas
	1 *who/which* clause (w/w)	1 end mark
	2 adverb clauses (AC)	2 usage
	1 *that* clause (that)	1 unclear pronoun
	5 subject-verb pairs (s v)	
	1 opener	

peering fiercely into his beady black eyes Mowgli

declared a new law who stated that he was free

to live as he pleased because he had always been

their loyal leader

Rewrite It! ____

____

____

____

____

Read It!	**Mark It!**	**Fix It!**	

Read It!	Mark It!	Fix It!
1 vocabulary	3 coordinating conjunctions (cc)	1 capital
	1 <u>prepositional phrase</u>	? commas
	2 [main clauses]	1 end mark
	1 adverb clause (AC)	2 apostrophes
	3 subject-verb pairs (s v)	2 usage
	1 opener	

as Mowgli **struck** right and left with the flaming

branch spark's sting the wolves fur and they

flee howling and wailing

Rewrite It! ______________________________________

____

____

____

Read It!	**Mark It!**	**Fix It!**
1 vocabulary	2 coordinating conjunctions (cc)	1 indent
	3 <u>prepositional phrases</u>	2 capitals
	2 [main clauses]	? commas
	1 *who/which* clause (w/w)	2 end marks
	3 subject-verb pairs (s v)	1 number
	2 openers	1 hyphen
		1 usage
		1 unclear pronoun

by **dusk** only Akela Bagheera and 12 well known

wolves who have bravely stood with him remained

looking tenderly at Mowgli Akela bowed his head

and thanked him

Rewrite It! ____

____

____

____

Read It!	**Mark It!**	**Fix It!**	Day 4

Read It!

1 vocabulary

Mark It!

1 coordinating conjunction (cc)
2 [main clauses]
1 *that* clause (that)
3 subject-verb pairs (s v)
1 opener

Fix It!

1 indent
1 capital
? commas
1 end mark
1 usage
1 unclear pronoun

strangely something newly began to hurt him inside

and he **blurted** out that he did not wish to leave his

familiar beloved jungle

Rewrite It! ____

____

____

____

Review It!

Unnecessary Commas

Using the list below, explain why the comma is wrong.

A	MC cc 2nd verb	**F**	*that* clause
B	a and b	**G**	#2 opener < 5 words
C	essential *who/which*	**H**	#3 opener modifies verb
D	strong interjection!	**I**	MC AC
E	cumulative adjectives	**J**	before prep phrase

C The twelve wolves, who stood with Mowgli, knew him well.

_____ Four had grown up with Mowgli, in the cave.

_____ Mother Wolf, and Father Wolf were two more.

_____ Thunder, Claw, and Howler were grateful, that Mowgli removed thorns.

_____ Wolfgang prized Mowgli's fishing skill, and respected his intelligence.

_____ During one debate, several wolves said Mowgli would protect them.

_____ Accurately, Mowgli could grasp man's thinking.

_____ Silver enjoyed their sport, although she couldn't hold Mowgli's stare.

_____ Fang admired how quickly the hairless, young cub learned.

_____ "Wow,! You can distinguish an owl's hoot!" she told Mowgli.

Read It!	**Mark It!**	**Fix It!**
1 vocabulary	1 coordinating conjunction (cc)	1 indent
	2 <u>prepositional phrases</u>	3 capitals
	4 [main clauses]	? commas
	1 adverb clause (AC)	2 quotation marks
	5 subject-verb pairs (s v)	3 end marks
	1 opener	3 usage

as warm salty tears poured down his cheeks

he was **confused** and he cried for help oh

Bagheera what was this wetness is he dying

Rewrite It! ____

____

____

____

Read It!	**Mark It!**	**Fix It!**
1 vocabulary	1 coordinating conjunction (cc)	1 indent
	1 <u>prepositional phrase</u>	2 capitals
	4 [main clauses]	? commas
	2 *that* clauses (that)	4 quotation marks
	6 subject-verb pairs (s v)	2 end marks
		1 apostrophe
		1 usage

those are only tears replied Bagheera clearly

your tears **confirm** that youre a man so now you

know that you does not belong in the jungle

Rewrite It! _______________________________________

____

____

____

Read It! | **Mark It!** | **Fix It!**

1 vocabulary	1 coordinating conjunction (cc)	1 indent
	1 <u>prepositional phrase</u>	2 capitals
	2 [main clauses]	? commas
	1 *who/which* clause (w/w)	2 end marks
	1 adverb clause (AC)	1 apostrophe
	1 *that* clause (that)	1 number
	5 subject-verb pairs (s v)	1 hyphen
	2 openers	

feeling that his heart would break Mowgli sobbed

when his tear's finally dried he **determined** to tell

his jungle family goodbye and to begin the 5 mile trek

to the village which would be his new home

Rewrite It! ____

____

____

____

Read It!	**Mark It!**	**Fix It!**	Day 4
1 vocabulary	4 <u>prepositional phrases</u>	1 indent	
	2 [main clauses]	5 capitals	
	1 *who/which* clause (w/w)	? commas	
	1 adverb clause (AC)	2 end marks	
	1 *that* clause (that)	1 apostrophe	
	5 subject-verb pairs (s v)	1 number	
	2 openers	1 unclear pronoun	

at the entrance of the cave he cried on mother

wolfs coat while the 6 brokenhearted cubs moaned

father wolf whose eyes were moist quietly watched

in **sorrow** wishing that he could stay

Rewrite It! ____

____

____

____

Review It!

Fill in the blanks below with different parts of speech in order to create a silly story about a creature Mowgli knew.

After you have completed the list on this page, transfer your words to the blanks in the story on page 181.

2 adjectives   _______________ _______________

1 noun (food)   _______________

2 nouns   _______________ _______________

1 adverb   _______________

1 noun (food)   _______________

1 speaking verb   _______________

2 adjectives   _______________ _______________

1 adverb   _______________

1 noun (food)   _______________

1 adjective   _______________

1 verb   _______________

1 speaking verb   _______________

1 adverb   _______________

1 verb   _______________

1 noun (time)   _______________

1 adjective   _______________

1 number   _______________

1 adverb   _______________

1 speaking verb   _______________

1 noun   _______________

1 noun (place)   _______________

Read It!	**Mark It!**	**Fix It!**
1 vocabulary	2 <u>prepositional phrases</u>	1 indent
	1 [main clause]	1 capital
	1 adverb clause (AC)	? commas
	2 subject-verb pairs (s v)	1 end mark
	1 opener	1 usage

pleading for him to visit often Mother Wolf sniffled

because herself had loved him as her own cub

Rewrite It! ______________________________

____

____

____

Read It!	Mark It!	Fix It!	Day 2

<table>
<tr><td>1 vocabulary</td><td>2 coordinating conjunctions (cc)</td><td>3 capitals</td></tr>
<tr><td></td><td>1 <u>prepositional phrase</u></td><td>? commas</td></tr>
<tr><td></td><td>3 [main clauses]</td><td>2 end marks</td></tr>
<tr><td></td><td>1 that clause (that)</td><td>1 apostrophe</td></tr>
<tr><td></td><td>4 subject-verb pairs (s v)</td><td>2 usage</td></tr>
<tr><td></td><td>2 openers</td><td></td></tr>
</table>

Mowgli assured her that he would certain return

he would always be thankful for she and father wolfs

generosity and he asked them never to forget him

Rewrite It! ____

____

____

____

____

Read It!	**Mark It!**	**Fix It!**
1 vocabulary	1 coordinating conjunction (cc)	1 indent
	2 <u>prepositional phrases</u>	3 capitals
	3 [main clauses]	? commas
	1 *who/which* clause (w/w)	3 end marks
	1 adverb clause (AC)	2 usage
	5 subject-verb pairs (s v)	
	3 openers	

as the bright orange sun rose Mowgli turned his

back on his childhood friends his adopted family and

his jungle playground he hurried down the hillside

to meet the strange beings which were called men

they are his **kin**

Rewrite It! ____

____

____

____

____

Read It!	**Mark It!**	**Fix It!**
1 vocabulary	3 <u>prepositional phrases</u>	2 capitals
	2 [main clauses]	? commas
	1 *that* clause (that)	2 end marks
	3 subject-verb pairs (s v)	
	2 openers	

as a stranger his feelings were **varied** finally Mowgli

was ready to take his place among men knowing

he would experience new adventures in the village

Rewrite It! ____

____

____

____

Learn It!

Use the words you chose on page 175 to complete the story.

The Jackal

by ______________________
your name

The jackal Tabaq was a ______________ creature. The wolves hated him because he made
_______adjective_______

mischief, told ______________ lies, and ate ______________ and pieces of ______________
_______adjective_______   _____noun (food)_____   _____noun_____

from the garbage. Sometimes he ran through the jungle biting ______________ in his way.
                                                              _____noun_____

One day Tabaq ______________ sniffed around the wolves' cave, hoping to be invited in
_______adverb_______

for some ______________. He ______________ to Father Wolf, "May ______________ luck
_____noun (food)_____   ___speaking verb___   _______adjective_______

go with you, oh ______________ Chief of the Wolves. May you always remember those who
_______adjective_______

are ______________ hungry."
_______adverb_______

Father Wolf recognized false flattery. "Look inside, but there is no food."

"Perhaps no ______________ for a wolf, but a ______________ person like myself can
_____noun (food)_____   _______adjective_______

feast on little." Tabaq ______________ into the cave, which was where he found a bone.
                       _______verb_______

Now, Tabaq knew that the wolves disliked Shere Khan. Meanly he ______________,
                                                              ___speaking verb___

"The Great Tiger has ______________ moved his hunting grounds. He plans to
                     _______adverb_______

______________ in this area for the next ______________. He told me so."
_______verb_______   _____noun (time)_____

Father Wolf became ______________ and enraged. "He has no right to change his hunting
                   _______adjective_______

grounds! He will frighten all the game within ______________ miles!"
                                              _______number_______

Tabaq ______________ ignored Father Wolf's anger. "Shall I tell him how grateful you
      _______adverb_______

are?" he ______________ and then slunk away.
         ___speaking verb___

A few days later, Shere Khan hunted in that area. It was a human being he was after, not

______________. This would be Mowgli's first experience in ______________.
_____noun_____   ____noun (place)____

Appendices

Mowgli and Shere Khan

Shere Khan was a tiger who lived near the vast Wainganga River in central India. The tiger could not capture wild game because he was lame in one foot from birth, so he attacked defenseless cattle instead. Shere Khan did not limit himself to cattle. Sometimes he hunted man.

The law of the jungle forbade the killing of man. If anyone harmed a human, it would endanger every beast in the jungle. The desperate villagers feared the beasts. They would send elephants and men with guns and torches into the jungle to kill them.

Shere Khan ignored the law of the jungle and hunted a boy. A toddler had strayed from his village.

Shere Khan's distant roar alerted Father Wolf to trouble. He paced angrily. Father Wolf was worried. Shere Khan was hunting again. His hunting would lead man to retaliate. With great apprehension Father Wolf paced. A small hairless creature wandered into the shallow cave and joined the six cubs and their mother. Until that day Father Wolf had never seen a man's cub. He stared in amazement at the puny child.

Without any warning Shere Khan appeared at the entrance of the cave but could not fit through the opening. He wanted the man's cub to come out.

Mother Wolf shook herself. She stood up, snarled, and glared at Shere Khan. She was furious. She growled, "The man's cub, who is now mine, lives here! He shall run with the pack and hunt with the pack. He will grow up and hunt you!"

Shere Khan, who had lost the argument, left in frustration. Mother Wolf planned to raise this man's cub in addition to her six cubs. Because of his looks she named him Mowgli, which means frog. She loved him for his unusual boldness, his comical expressions, and his playful spirit. Father Wolf, who was more practical, feared for Mowgli's acceptance. He would need approval from two members of the pack.

Finally, the night of the annual meeting came. The entire pack gathered around when it was dusk. The summer moon was full. The air was still. After the announcements Father Wolf presented Mowgli, who was squatting in the dirt as he quietly played a game with rocks and sticks.

At the edge of the group, Shere Khan paced and snarled while other members talked. "The man's cub is mine. Give him to me now!" he threatened viciously.

The lone gray wolf, who was named Akela, led the pack because he was considerably strong. "Who speaks for this cub?" he cried out.

Quietly a sleepy brown bear, who was named Baloo, addressed the wolves. "Do you mean the man's cub? Mowgli learns from me. I'll speak for him."

Akela asked if anyone else would claim him.

Bagheera, who was the black panther, dropped into the circle and looked boldly at the pack. "Although I'm not a member of your pack," he began, "the laws of the jungle allow anyone in the jungle to purchase the life of a cub for a price. This cub, who lives with the pack, is innocent. I've killed a fat bull. Take it as payment to preserve his life."

The pack's only interest was that they were given a free meal. Eagerly they cried, "Who cares? He'll die in the chilly winter rains or scorch in the summer sun."

As he withdrew from the pack, Shere Khan, who muttered thickly under his breath, was disappointed that the ugly human creature was still not his.

For the next ten years, Mowgli learned the ways of the jungle. Before long he could detect every bird's note and every animal's track. Baloo taught him to climb for honey. In his leisure Mowgli happily swam in the jungle's pools when he felt dirty or hot. In fear Mowgli awkwardly held the trees' branches, which spread in all directions. With practice he swung and flung himself through them like a monkey.

As he learned the ways of the jungle, he grew tough. He was happy and carefree. He only worried about his stomach's next meal. He discovered that the wolves would drop their gaze if he stared directly at their eyes. For fun Mowgli did it on purpose. On other occasions he would pull thorns from his friends' sore paws. This eased their suffering.

Mowgli would watch the villagers' huts in the evenings, but he mistrusted people because they cruelly set traps for his friends. Akela aged, and Shere Khan waited. Craftily Shere Khan, who rewarded his followers, fed scraps to the younger wolves because they wanted food.

At times Shere Khan would ask, "Why are such impressive hunters as yourselves content that you are led by one dying wolf and a man's cub?" At other times he would comment, "Hah! You fear to look at Mowgli's eyes." Angrily the young wolves, who felt embarrassed, would grumble.

Urgently Bagheera, who had eyes and ears everywhere, warned Mowgli. "Shere Khan hates you and plans to harm you. How often have I told you this?"

Mowgli shrugged. "Pooh! You've told me, and I've heard you hundreds of times. I am not scared and won't hide, Bagheera."

"You should be concerned because you're in danger, Mowgli. Baloo, the pack, and even the silly deer know that Shere Khan is hateful."

Bagheera argued that Shere Khan selfishly manipulated the younger wolves and told them that men's cubs had no place in the pack. Although Shere Khan would not kill Mowgli in the jungle, Akela was simply too old to control the tiger's response whenever he became aggressive.

As Bagheera paced, he hesitated and said, "In two years' time you will be a grown man, Mowgli. Shere Khan has taught the wolves. They listen to him."

"Shouldn't a man run with his brothers?" Mowgli reasoned. "Truly, I have obeyed the laws of the jungle and have helped the pack."

Bagheera, who stretched himself, shut his eyes. Since Mowgli was oblivious to their hatred, he decided that he should share his secret. "Mowgli, feel under my jaw, which reveals my secrets."

Under his chin Bagheera's muscles were hidden beneath his black hair. Mowgli felt a small jagged spot and wondered about it. Bagheera confessed that nobody in the jungle knew that he bore the mark of the chain. That spot was its sign and would be with him forever. Because he was born in captivity, he had never lived in the jungle, which should have been his home. That was the reason that he'd paid for Mowgli to join the pack.

Bagheera explained, "Miserably my mother died in the king's palace. In that place men fed the captives and me until I finally understood that I was stronger than man." Breaking the lock with one blow of his paw, Bagheera had escaped from the palace when he realized that the chains couldn't hold him. Hoping cautiously that Mowgli would understand, Bagheera made his point. "Mowgli, you must return to your people, or you'll be killed."

Pacing in distress, Mowgli replied, "You're confusing me. What have I done that anyone would want to kill me?"

Answering firmly, Bagheera ordered, "Look at me, Mowgli."

Mowgli, who wanted to understand, obeyed and steadily looked at him in the eyes.

Looking down after a minute, the panther turned away. "Although I love you, even I can't hold your intense gaze."

In fact, it was true. Others avoided Mowgli because they could not stare back. They knew that he was smart and could accomplish things that they couldn't. Painfully Mowgli responded that he didn't know those things, which made him angry, sad, and disappointed.

"By the way that you behave," Bagheera warned, "they recognize that you're a man. When Akela has an unsuccessful hunt, the pack will attack you." Suddenly Bagheera added, "I have an idea that might work. From the men's huts in the village, take some of their red flower, which glows brightly."

He knew its potential. Because the animals dreaded fire, they had over one hundred different names for it. Red flower was one.

Obeying Bagheera, Mowgli left and raced through the jungle. During his run he heard the pack's cry, and he grew anxious.

He heard laughter from the young wolves as they taunted their aging leader. "Attack the elk, Akela! Show your strength!"

Mowgli heard the snap of Akela's teeth and then his cry as the elk kicked him. Akela howled in anger, missing his kill. Fearfully Mowgli dashed, descending from the hills into the farmland near the village. As he ran, the shrill sounds, which terrified him, grew fainter.

Beneath the window of a hut, Mowgli crouched, thinking about Bagheera's wise words. By tomorrow the wolves' claws would reach him. He pressed his face to the window, spotting a fire in a large hole. During the night a woman fed it with unfamiliar black lumps and gently blew on them.

As the cool morning mist appeared, Mowgli saw that a child entered the hut. The young boy grabbed a pot, placed six black lumps in it, and left to milk the cows. Mowgli concluded that he obviously had nothing to fear if a helpless human child, who was just a cub, could carry it.

Sneaking around the hut's corner, he grabbed the pot from the hand of the astounded small boy and left immediately. He now had the source of the red flower. Carefully Mowgli blew into the pot as the woman had done, understanding that he'd have to feed the mysterious round lumps constantly.

Scrambling up the jagged, rocky hill, Mowgli spotted Bagheera, who eagerly hailed him. Mowgli ran toward him. Bagheera informed Mowgli that Akela had missed his kill and that Mowgli was now in danger. During the night the senseless, cruel wolves would kill Akela and hunt for Mowgli.

Mowgli showed the dingy, dirty pot with its glowing red coals, exclaiming that they would inevitably protect him. Bagheera praised Mowgli. He explained that dry, brittle branches blossomed dangerously when men placed them into the burning red flower.

At the group's afternoon meeting, Mowgli arrived, feeling capable and unafraid. The animals who wanted to kill him whispered impatiently. Signaling that it was time to begin the meeting, Akela stood on a flat, square rock, which was called Council Rock. The wolves who followed Shere Khan circled around him and waited for him to speak. Silently Bagheera lay beside Mowgli, who clutched the clay fire pot.

When the pack was quiet, Shere Khan started to speak, but Mowgli interrupted him, challenging the wolves who threatened Akela. "Cowards, are you ruled by a tiger? Must you obey this clumsy, overgrown cat, who is no better than a bully? You could have shown courage and kindness!"

Glaring at him, some yelled, "Keep silent, man's cub!"

Others begged, "Let him speak. He's kept our law." The tension grew.

Wearily Akela stated that for twelve successful years he faithfully led his pack, proving his strength and skill. Until last night he had always led them to the kill, and never had anyone been hurt. Since he missed his attack yesterday, the jungle's firm law stated that they could kill him now, but by the same law they must approach one at a time.

At that moment no one spoke because no solitary wolf wanted to fight Akela to the death.

Breaking the silence, Shere Khan roared at the wolves. "Who cares about the old wolf? It's the man's cub whom I despise. Unless you give him to me now, I will never again share fresh, succulent bones with you."

Rising to his feet, Akela made an announcement. He stated that Mowgli had shared their food and had tended their sick. Recently, he'd driven game for them.

Growling menacingly, Bagheera threatened that the loyal wolves and he would fight for Mowgli, whom he had purchased with a bull many years ago.

Grumbling loudly, the pack did not care about the bull, whose dry, brittle bones had been lying around for a decade. Because Bagheera sought justice, he asked the wolves, whose vows had been important, if they still cared about their vows. Did they choose for themselves, or did they obey this killer of cattle?

The tiger protested that wolves could not run with a man's cub. He demanded that they give him Mowgli, whom he had hated for so long.

With tenderness Akela replied that in everything but blood Mowgli had been their brother. He'd maintained the law of the jungle better than any of them had.

The wolves did not admit that Shere Khan influenced them. Secretly they had crept into the villages of men, whose cattle they had killed.

With sorrow Akela knew he had to die, but if they restored the man's cub to his village, he would not fight them when the time came. He requested they consider his plan. If they agreed, they would save some lives and would not shame the pack for the killing of an innocent human brother, who had been bought into the pack.

Complaining against Mowgli, most of the wolves gathered around Shere Khan, whose tail was beginning to whip furiously.

Murmuring to Mowgli, Bagheera encouraged him to stand for justice. They would fight for Mowgli's and Akela's lives and teach Shere Khan a lesson.

Inwardly Mowgli felt rage and sorrow because no wolf had ever shown him such hatred. Holding out the warm fire pot, Mowgli was empowered by the burning coals. "Cease this foolish talk!" he ordered. "To my life's end I would have stayed a wolf, but I know you speak the truth, declaring that I am a man. Because I now comprehend I'm human, I no longer call you brothers. Look! I hold the mighty red flower, which you fear."

At once he threw the glowing red coals on the ground, igniting some dried moss. Fearfully the wolves, whose hair stood on end, backed away. Thrusting a dry, dead branch into the fire until it lit, Mowgli whirled it above his head, looked at Bagheera, and moved toward the cowering wolves.

"Since you control the pack, Mowgli," whispered Bagheera, "you can save Akela from death. He has consistently been your friend, so now you can repay him for his kindness."

Standing alone, Mowgli held the burning branch high in the air. The shadows quivered. Akela hoped Mowgli would be merciful. He looked straight at him.

Because Mowgli was no longer welcome in the jungle, he had to leave, but he pledged that he would be more compassionate than those cold-blooded wolves. Mowgli, who was their self-confident brother, wouldn't betray them to men as they had cruelly betrayed him.

In addition, Mowgli knew he still had one debt to pay. Boldly he approached Shere Khan, who was staring nervously at the flames, and grabbed the strong-willed tiger by the hair on his chin. With his ears against his head, Shere Khan frantically shut his eyes, whimpering because of the blazing-hot branch.

"This coward confidently bragged he would destroy me at the next meeting because he had not killed me when I was a cub. As a man I will not tolerate rude, nasty cowards and self-serving bullies. If you move a whisker, you will feel these flames!"

Holding Shere Khan's chin, Mowgli listened as the tiger trembled and whined. "Leave now!" Mowgli commanded. "Never come back, or I'll stop you forever."

Growling in terror, Shere Khan fled into the jungle.

Mowgli looked at Akela, whom he respected. He then turned, positioning himself between Akela and the other wolves.

Peering fiercely into their beady black eyes, Mowgli declared a new law, which stated that Akela was free to live as he pleased because he had always been their loyal leader. As Mowgli struck right and left with the flaming branch, sparks stung the wolves' fur, and they fled, howling and wailing.

By dusk only Akela, Bagheera, and twelve well-known wolves who had bravely stood with Mowgli remained. Looking tenderly at Mowgli, Akela bowed his head and thanked him.

Strangely, something new began to hurt Mowgli inside, and he blurted out that he did not wish to leave his familiar, beloved jungle.

As warm salty tears poured down his cheeks, he was confused, and he cried for help. "Oh, Bagheera, what is this wetness? Am I dying?"

"Those are only tears," replied Bagheera. "Clearly, your tears confirm that you're a man, so now you know that you do not belong in the jungle."

Feeling that his heart would break, Mowgli sobbed. When his tears finally dried, he determined to tell his jungle family goodbye and to begin the five-mile trek to the village, which would be his new home.

At the entrance of the cave, he cried on Mother Wolf's coat while the six brokenhearted cubs moaned. Father Wolf, whose eyes were moist, quietly watched in sorrow, wishing that Mowgli could stay.

Pleading for him to visit often, Mother Wolf sniffled because she had loved him as her own cub. Mowgli assured her that he would certainly return. He would always be thankful for her and Father Wolf's generosity, and he asked them never to forget him.

As the bright orange sun rose, Mowgli turned his back on his childhood friends, his adopted family, and his jungle playground. He hurried down the hillside to meet the strange beings who were called men. They were his kin. As a stranger his feelings were varied. Finally, Mowgli was ready to take his place among men, knowing he would experience new adventures in the village.

-ly Adverb

An **-ly adverb** dresses up writing because it creates a strong image or feeling.

Strong Verb

A **strong verb** dresses up writing because it creates a strong image or feeling. A strong verb is an action verb, never a linking or helping verb.

Quality Adjective

A **quality adjective** dresses up writing because it creates a strong image or feeling. A quality adjective is more specific than a weak adjective, which is overused, boring, or vague.

Pronoun

A **pronoun** replaces a noun in order to avoid repetition.

A **personal pronoun** takes the place of common and proper nouns. It should agree with its antecedent in number, person, and case.

A **reflexive pronoun** ends in -self or -selves and refers to the subject of the same sentence.

3 cases		Subjective function as	Objective function as	Possessive function as		Reflexive refers to
		subject subject complement	object of a preposition direct object indirect object	adjective	pronoun	subject of same sentence
2 numbers	3 persons					
singular	1st	I	me	my	mine	myself
	2nd	you	you	your	yours	yourself
	3rd	he, she, it	him, her, it	his, her, its	his, hers, its	himself, herself, itself
plural	1st	we	us	our	ours	ourselves
	2nd	you	you	your	yours	yourselves
	3rd	they	them	their	theirs	themselves

A **relative pronoun** begins a dependent *who/which* clause. The pronoun *who* has three forms: *who* (subjective), *whom* (objective), *whose* (possessive).

who, whom, whose, which, that

An **interrogative pronoun** is used to ask a question.

what, whatever, which, whichever, who, whoever, whom, whose

A **demonstrative pronoun** points to a particular person or thing. When a word on the demonstrative list is placed before a noun, it functions as an adjective, not a pronoun.

this, that, these, those

An **indefinite pronoun** is not definite. It does not refer to any particular person or thing. When a word on the indefinite list is placed before a noun, it functions as an adjective, not a pronoun.

Singular and Plural	Plural	Singular			
all	both		each	much	one
any	few	another	either	neither	other
more	many	anybody	everybody	nobody	somebody
most	others	anyone	everyone	no one	someone
none	own	anything	everything	nothing	something
some	several	anywhere	everywhere	nowhere	somewhere

Preposition

A **preposition** starts a phrase that shows the relationship between a noun or pronoun and another word in the sentence. **PATTERN preposition + noun (no verb)**

This is not an exhaustive list. When in doubt, consult a dictionary.

aboard	amid	beneath	down	into	opposite	throughout	up
about	among	beside	during	like	out	to	upon
above	around	besides	except	minus	outside	toward	with
according to	as	between	for	near	over	under	within
across	at	beyond	from	of	past	underneath	without
after	because of	by	in	off	regarding	unlike	
against	before	concerning	inside	on	since	until	
along	behind	despite	instead of	onto	through	unto	

Verb

A **verb** shows action, links the subject to another word, or helps another verb.

An **action verb** shows action or ownership.

A **linking verb** links the subject to a noun or adjective.

am, is, are, was, were, be, being, been (be verbs)

seem, become, appear, grow, remain, taste, sound, smell, feel, look (verbs dealing with the senses)

A **helping verb** helps an action verb or a linking verb.

am, is, are, was, were, be, being, been (be verbs)

have, has, had, do, does, did, may, might, must, can, will, shall, could, would, should

Conjunction

A **conjunction** connects words, phrases, or clauses.

An **coordinating conjunction** (cc) connects the same type of words, phrases, or clauses.

FANBOYS   for, and, nor, but, or, yet, so

A **subordinating conjunction** (www word) connects an adverb clause to a main clause.

www.asia.b   when, while, where, as, since, if although, because

before, after, until, unless, whenever, whereas, than

FIX-L4-S
ISBN 978-1-62341-363-7